Revised Edition

Travel English at Your Fingertips

Takuji Shimada   Bill Benfield

photographs by
iStockphoto
Dreamstime

音声ファイルのダウンロード／ストリーミング

CD マーク表示がある箇所は、音声を弊社 HP より無料でダウンロード／ストリーミングすることができます。トップページのバナーをクリックし、書籍検索してください。書籍詳細ページに音声ダウンロードアイコンがございますのでそちらから自習用音声としてご活用ください。

https://www.seibido.co.jp

Travel English at Your Fintertips —Revised Edition—
実用観光英語―改訂新版―

Copyright © 2019 by Takuji Shimada, Bill Benfield

All rights reserved; no part of this publication may be reproduced, stored in a retrieval system, or transmitted in any form or by any means, electronic, mechanical, photocopying, recording, or otherwise, without the prior written permission of the author.

はしがき

　本書は、*Travel English at Your Fingertips*『実用観光英語』の改訂新版です。本書の初版は、海外旅行でスムーズに自分の意思を伝えるための英語運用能力の習得を目指した総合教材として、2001 年に発行され、これまで多くの学習者のみなさんにご好評頂きました。この間、世界情勢は大きく変化し、海外旅行の形態も様変わりしました。たとえば、2008 年 9 月に起きたリーマン・ショック後、トラベラーズ・チェックが全くと言っていいほど使われなくなりましたし、インターネットやスマートフォンの普及により、旅行中に絵葉書を送ったり、国際電話をかけたりすることもほとんどなくなったと言っていいでしょう。スマホ 1 つあれば、ホテルやチケットの予約もインターネット上で簡単にできますし、道に迷っても、簡単に自分の所在地を特定できます。

　このような状況を鑑み、改訂新版では、現代の海外旅行の現状に合わせるために内容を大幅に刷新しました。国際電話、郵便局、銀行、道案内等のユニットは削除する一方、新たに Substitution Drills を加えることで、各ユニットの充実を図りました。海外旅行中に頻繁に出くわす場面で必要な「読む」、「聞く」、「話す」能力を効果的に学習できるように配慮してありますので、本書で取り上げた表現を身につければ、海外旅行がいっそう楽しめるようになるでしょうし、パッケージツアーなどでは味わえない自分だけのオリジナル旅行を満喫できるようになるはずです。

　本書はアメリカ旅行の出発から帰国までの場面を扱った全 15 ユニットで構成されており、各ユニットでは以下に挙げる 8 つの異なるタスクを行うことによって、必要語彙、表現などを習得していきます。さまざまな形式のタスクをくり返しこなしていくことになるので、無理なく必要な表現を身につけることが出来るはずです。

1. Pre-Listening Exercise

　各ユニットの Dialog または Monolog に出てくる語句の中から、特に観光英語特有のものを中心にまとめてあります。日本語訳とのマッチング形式のタスクを通して、語彙、表現を学習します。

2. Listening Comprehension

　各ユニットの Dialog または Monolog を聴いて内容が把握できているかどうか確認します。

3. Dictation

　各ユニットの Dialog または Monolog の穴埋め問題です。カッコの数は、学習者が過度の負担を感じないよう 20 個以下に制限し、カッコに入る語は、特に習得すべき表現や聞き間違えの多い数字が中心になっています。

4. Related Dialogs

　各ユニットの話題に関連した 3 種類の短い Dialog または Monolog を聴いて答える問題で、より多くの関連する Dialog（Monolog）を聴くことによって英語表現力を高めることを目的としています。TOEIC 形式の問題を念頭において作成しました。

5. Useful Expression

　役立つ表現を Dictation の形式で学習するための作業です。Dialog や Monolog で使用された表現を少し変えたものや、応用したものが中心になっていますが、そのユニットで扱えなかった他の重要表現も含まれています。

6. Substitution Drills

　各ユニットで扱った重要表現の置き換え練習です。音声の後に続いて口頭ですらすら言えるようになるまで練習して下さい。

7. Translation

　各ユニットで扱った重要表現が習得できたかを和文英訳により確認します。

8. Reading for Information / Vocabulary

　各ユニットの最後に、Reading for Information あるいは Vocabulary の練習問題を加えました。Reading for Information は絵や表、旅行パンフレット、地図などを使用して必要な情報を得るという作業です。Dialog や Monolog など音声からは得られない情報をすばやく読み取る作業を通して、海外旅行中に出くわす文字情報に対処するための能力向上を目指します。また、Vocabulary では、問題を通して、その Unit では扱わなかった重要語彙、表現の習得を目標にしています。

　以上のタスクを根気よくこなしていくことで、海外旅行に必要な語彙や表現に親しみ、これまで以上に海外旅行が楽しめるようになっていただきたいと願っています。

　最後になりましたが、本書の企画、出版にあたり、成美堂編集部の田村栄一氏と佐藤公雄氏に大変お世話になりました。ここに感謝の意を表します。

筆　者

Contents

UNIT 1 In-Flight Announcements *1*

UNIT 2 At Immigration and Customs *7*

UNIT 3 Getting to a Hotel *13*

UNIT 4 Checking into a Hotel *19*

UNIT 5 Checking in without a Reservation *25*

UNIT 6 At a Restaurant *31*

UNIT 7 Taking the Subway *37*

UNIT 8 At a Fast-Food Restaurant *43*

UNIT 9 Hotel Service *49*

UNIT 10 Booking a Tour *55*

UNIT 11 Health Care *61*

UNIT 12 Shopping *67*

UNIT 13 Making Complaints *73*

UNIT 14 Dealing with Problems *79*

UNIT 15 At the Airport *85*

UNIT 1
In-Flight Announcements

1 Pre-Listening Exercise

Guess what these words mean and match the appropriate meaning given in Japanese.

☐ a. take off   ☐ b. fasten (your) seat belt   ☐ c. baggage (= luggage)
☐ d. overhead compartment   ☐ e. upright position   ☐ f. electronic devices
☐ g. laptop   ☐ h. cell phone   ☐ i. cruise   ☐ j. at an altitude of ~
☐ k. tailwind   ☐ l. ahead of schedule   ☐ m. cooperate
☐ n. descend   ☐ o. beverage   ☐ p. destination

```
1. 電子機器    2. 降下する    3. 巡航（一定の高度と速度で飛行）する
4. 座席上の共用収納棚    5. 手荷物    6. シートベルトを締める    7. 飲料
8. 目的地    9. 離陸する    10. 携帯電話    11. 直立位置    12. ノートパソコン
13. ～の高度で    14. 追い風、順風    15. 予定より早く
16.（状況が）うまく進展する
```

2 Comprehension Questions

 1-02, 03

(A) Listen to the first in-flight announcement and choose the best answer for each question.

Q1. What flight is the announcement for?

    a) AA60   b) JA16   c) NH60

Q2. What are the passengers supposed to do?

    a) fasten their seatbelts

    b) put their baggage under their seats

    c) use a portable PC

1

(B) Listen to the second in-flight announcement and choose the best answer for each question.

Q3. How high and fast is the aircraft currently flying?

    a) 3,300 meters at a speed of 350 miles per hour

    b) 13,000 feet at a speed of 400 miles per hour

    c) 33,000 feet at a speed of 400 miles per hour

Q4. What is the weather in London like?

    a) sunny and warm

    b) warm and windy

    c) clear and sunny

3 Dictation

 1-04, 05

Fill in the blanks while listening to the two announcements.

A. In-Flight Announcement One

Ladies and gentlemen, welcome (¹   ) Flight 60 to Dallas. We are expected to take off (²   ) about seven minutes. Please (³   ) your seat belts at this time and (⁴   ) all baggage in the overhead compartments or (⁵   ) the seats in front of you. We ask that your seats and tray tables are in the (⁶   ) position for takeoff. Please turn off all personal electronic devices, including laptops and cell phones. Thank you for (⁷   ) (⁸   ) Airlines. Enjoy your flight.

B. In-Flight Announcement Two

Good afternoon, passengers. This is your captain speaking. First, I'd like to welcome everyone on British Airways Flight 1594. We are (⁹   ) cruising at an altitude of 33,000 feet at an (¹⁰   ) of 400 miles per hour. The weather is fine and with the (¹¹   ) on our side, we are expecting to land in London approximately 20 minutes (¹²   )

UNIT 1 In-Flight Announcements

of schedule. The weather in London is sunny and warm, with a high of 23 (¹³   ). If the weather cooperates, we should get a beautiful night (¹⁴   ) of the city as we descend.

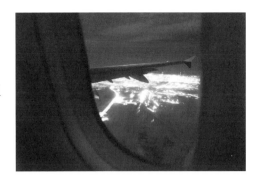

4 Related Monologs

 1-06, 07, 08

Listen to the three monologs and choose the best answer for each question.

Monolog One

Question: **Why do the passengers have to return to their seats?**

   a. Because the plane may drop suddenly
   b. Because the plane is flying faster than usual
   c. Because the plane is ready to land

| turbulence 「乱気流」

Monolog Two

Question: **What are the passengers most likely to receive soon?**

   a. breakfast
   b. headsets
   c. drinks

| flight attendant 「客室乗務員」

Monolog Three

Question: **What time is it in San Francisco?**

   a. a quarter to ten
   b. a quarter to eleven
   c. a quarter past eleven

| local time 「現地時間」 Fahrenheit 「カ氏」

5 Useful Expressions 1-09

Listen and write the sentences.

1. ....

2. ....

3. ....

4. ....

6 Substitution Drills  1-10, 11, 12

Complete the substitution drill in the following way.

(1) Thank you for <u>flying Japan Airlines flight 60</u> to <u>Los Angeles</u>.

> **Example:** taking American Airlines flight 176 – Dallas
> ➡ Thank you for taking American Airlines flight 176 to Dallas.

a) taking American Airlines flight 176 – Dallas
b) using All Nippon Airways flight 186 – Honolulu
c) choosing Delta Air Lines flight 2210 – Seattle

(2) Please <u>put your baggage</u> <u>under the seat in front of you</u>.

> **Example:** store your carry-ons – in the overhead bin
> ➡ Please store your carry-ons in the overhead bin.

a) store your carry-ons – in the overhead bin
b) stow your hand baggage – under the seat in front of you
c) put your bags – in the overhead compartment

| store = stow 「詰め込む ; しまい込む」 overhead bin = overhead compartment

UNIT 1 In-Flight Announcements

(3) We're <u>expected to take off</u> <u>shortly</u>.

> **Example:** scheduled to land – in about 30 minutes
> ➡ We're scheduled to land in about 30 minutes.

  a) scheduled to land – in about 30 minutes

  b) expected to depart – in about 15 minutes

  c) supposed to reach New York – about 20 minutes behind schedule

  | behind schedule「予定より遅れて」

7 Translation

Put the following Japanese sentences into English.

1. 当機はおよそ 15 分後に離陸する予定でございます。

_____

2. 手荷物は座席上の共用収納棚や前の座席の下にご収納ください。

_____

3. 当機は、今から 3 時間後にサンフランシスコ国際空港に到着予定です。

_____

4. 安全のため、飛行機が完全に止まるまで、席に座ったままでいてください。

_____

5

8 Vocabulary

Fill in the blanks with the words and phrases provided below.

1. Your departure time has moved (   ).
   出発時間が早くなりました。

2. I'm afraid you're in the (   ) seat. Could you check your seat number?
   席が間違っているようですが。座席番号を確認していただけますか。

3. Is a meal (   ) on this flight?
   このフライトは食事が出ますか。

4. How do I (   ) the reading light?
   どうやって読書灯をつけるのですか。

5. Could I have a (   ) declaration form?
   税関申告書をいただけますか。

6. Could you tell me how to (   ) this form?
   この用紙の記入方法を教えていただけますか。

7. I'd (   ) have chicken than beef.
   ビーフよりもチキンをいただきたいのですが。

8. How many hours does it (   ) to get to New York?
   ニューヨークまで何時間かかりますか。

9. We're (   ) turbulence. Please fasten your seat belts.
   この先、気流の悪いところを通過します。シートベルトを締めてください。

10. It might be a (   ) ride.
    かなり揺れるかもしれません。

11. Are we arriving in New York (   )?
    ニューヨークには時間通りに到着しますか。

12. We're now 20 minutes (   ) schedule.
    予定より20分遅れています。

expecting	rather	take	wrong
bumpy	forward	served	behind
on time	fill out	turn on	customs

6

UNIT 2
At Immigration and Customs

1 Pre-Listening Exercise

Guess what these words mean and match the appropriate meaning given in Japanese.

☐ a. motion sickness ☐ b. purpose ☐ c. return ticket ☐ d. itinerary
☐ e. fingerprints ☐ f. declare ☐ g. all set ☐ h. inspection
☐ i. personal effects ☐ j. thumb ☐ k. intend to

1. 準備万端である；(手続き) 完了である	2. 親指	3. 身の回り品	4. 検査
5. 申告する 6. 目的 7. 帰りの切符	8. (～する) つもりである		9. 指紋
10. 乗り物酔い 11. 旅程			

2 Comprehension Questions 1-13, 14

(A) Listen to the conversation at immigration and choose the best answer for each question.

Q1. What did Hiroshi have to show to the immigration officer?

    a) his passport, customs declaration form, and return ticket

    b) his passport, return ticket, and money

    c) his passport, boarding pass, and return ticket

Q2. Which of the following did the officer NOT ask Hiroshi?

    a) where he will be staying

    b) how long he will be in the United States

    c) which airline he flew on

Q3. Where will Hiroshi be staying in the United States?

a) San Francisco and Los Angeles

b) San Francisco and New York City

c) Los Angeles and New York City

(B) Listen to the conversation at customs and choose the best answer for the question.

Q4. What does Hiroshi have in his bag?

a) some items for personal use

b) some alcoholic drinks

c) some plants and fruits

3 Dictation

CD 1-15, 16

Fill in the blanks while listening to the dialogs.

A. At Immigration

Officer: Good morning. May I see your passport and (^{1}) declaration form, please?

Hiroshi: Here you are.

Officer: What's the (^{2}) of your trip to the United States?

Hiroshi: Sightseeing.

Officer: How long do you (^{3}) to stay here?

Hiroshi: Three weeks.

Officer: What (^{4}) of the U.S. will you be visiting?

Hiroshi: San Francisco and New York City.

Officer: Do you have a return ticket?

Hiroshi: Sure. It's in my bag. ... Here you are.

Officer: Thank you. (^{5}) will you be staying?

Hiroshi: Oh, I'll be staying in several (^{6}) places. Here's my (^{7}).

[*Hiroshi shows his itinerary to the officer.*]

Officer: Thank you.

[*The officer returns it to Hiroshi.*]

UNIT 2   At Immigration and Customs

Press your right four fingers on the (^{8}).

Hiroshi: Sure.

Officer: Right (^{9}). Left four fingers. Left (^{10}).

[*Hiroshi follows the officer's instructions on fingerprinting.*]

[*The officer points at the camera.*]

Look at the camera. …

Thank you. Your passport and customs declaration form. You're all set.

Hiroshi: Thank you.

B. At Customs

Officer: Do you have anything to (^{11})?

Hiroshi: No, (^{12}).

Officer: What do you have in this bag?

Hiroshi: Only my personal (^{13}).

Officer: Please open your bag for (^{14}).

Hiroshi: All right.

Officer: What's this?

Hiroshi: My medicine for (^{15}) sickness.

Officer: Do you have any plants or fruit with you?

Hiroshi: No, I don't.

customs declaration form「税関申告書」

---

4 Related Dialogs

CD 1-17, 18, 19

Listen to the three dialogs and choose the best answer for each question.

Dialog One

Question: **How long will she be in the United States?**

   a. 2 weeks   **b.** 4 weeks   **c.** 6 weeks

attend「出席する、（学校）に行く」 intensive English program「集中英語プログラム」 last「続く」

Dialog Two

Question: **What did the woman forget to write down on the form?**

   a. the name of the airline and the flight number

   b. the name of the airline and the arrival time

   c. the name of the port of embarkation and the flight number

port of embarkation「搭乗地」

9

Dialog Three

Question: **About how much is the total value of his gifts?**

    a. $13   b. $18   c. $35

5 Useful Expressions

 1-20

Listen and write the sentences.

1. ....

2. ....

3. ....

4. ....

6 Substitution Drills

 1-21, 22, 23

Complete the substitution drill in the following way.

(1) How long <u>do you intend</u> to <u>stay here</u>?

> **Example:** do you plan – travel in the United States
> ➡ How long do you plan to travel in the United States?

    a) do you plan – travel in the United States

    b) does she want – stay in Los Angeles

    c) do they intend – study in the United States

UNIT 2 At Immigration and Customs

(2) **What part of <u>the United States</u> <u>will you be visiting</u>?**

> **Example:** France – will you be sightseeing in
> ➡ What part of France will you be sightseeing in?

a) France – will you be sightseeing in

b) Japan – are we going to visit

c) Hokkaido – will she be visiting

(3) **Do you have <u>anything</u> to <u>declare</u>?**

> **Example:** something hot - drink
> ➡ Do you have something hot to drink?

a) something hot – drink

b) anything else – say

c) any restaurants – recommend for dinner

7 Translation

Put the following Japanese sentences into English.

1. カナダへの入国目的は何ですか。

_____

2. 米国での滞在期間はどのくらいですか。

_____

3. 日本のどこを訪れる予定ですか。

_____

4. これは、私のノートパソコンの予備バッテリーです。

_____

5. 検査のために、あなたのスーツケースを開けてください。

_____

11

8 Reading for Information

Read the following information on immigration process and answer the questions below.

New Immigration Procedures

A new system for passport stamps will come into effect in May 2013. Under this new system, there will be two dates in your passport. One will show the date you arrived in the U.S., and the other, called the "admitted until" date, shows the date when your permitted period of stay expires.

When you arrive in the U.S. you will first be interviewed by a CBP officer — in other words, the immigration officer at your port of entry. This official will ask you several questions to determine whether you may be admitted to the country and, if so, for how long. These questions will include inquiries such as what the purpose of your visit is, how long you intend to remain in the country, where you will stay, and which country you normally reside in. When answering questions, you must be sure to keep your answers brief and relevant with no unnecessary details. It would probably be a good idea to prepare these answers in advance and write them down in a notebook or on a piece of paper.

Once you are given permission to enter the country, the CBP official will stamp your passport in the way mentioned above, with a date showing the duration of your permitted stay. For example, if you have a visitor visa, this may be six months. If you have an H1B/H4 visa, this period will be three years. It is important that you observe the expiration date as it is illegal to stay in the U.S. after that date.

Under the US-VISIT program, all non-U.S. citizens are required to be fingerprinted and photographed when entering the country.

> come into effect「〔法律などが〕有効になる；実施される」 permitted period「正式に許可された期間」
> expire「有効期限が切れる」 CBP = Customs and Border Protection「税関・国境警備局」
> port of entry「通関手続き地」 inquiry「質問」 reside in「住む；居住する」 relevant「関連のある；
> 適切な」 duration「期間」 illegal「違法の」

1. After May 2013, what indicates the date you arrived in the United States?

2. The CBP officer's stamp in your passport shows two dates. One of them is the date you entered the country. What does the other one indicate?

3. What questions may the CBP officer ask you during the interview?

4. How should your answers be during the inspection?

5. What is required of all non-U.S. citizens under the US-VISIT program?

UNIT 3
Getting to a Hotel

1 Pre-Listening Exercise

Guess what these words mean and match the appropriate meaning given in Japanese.

☐ **a.** tourist information center   ☐ **b.** downtown   ☐ **c.** abbreviation
☐ **d.** transit   ☐ **e.** depend on ~   ☐ **f.** less than   ☐ **g.** somewhere
☐ **h.** fare   ☐ **i.** signage   ☐ **j.** traffic

> 1. ～による；～次第である　2.（指示・警告の）看板，標識　3. ～未満の；～を下回る
> 4. 観光案内所　5. およそ～くらい　6. 略語　7. 乗車料金　8. 中心街
> 9. 運送，輸送　10. 交通（量），往来

2 Comprehension Questions

 1-24, 25

(A) Listen to the conversation between Hiroshi and a clerk at a tourist information center and choose the best answer for each question.

Q1. Where is Hiroshi headed for?

    a) the bus station　　**b)** the airport　　**c)** downtown

| head「～へ向かう」

Q2. What does BART stand for?

    a) Bay Area Rapid Transportation
    b) Bay Area Rapid Transport
    c) Bay Area Rapid Transit

| stand for = represent「～を表す」　transportation「輸送機関（手段）」

13

Q3. How long does it take to get to Powell by BART?

    a) about 15 minutes   **b)** about 30 minutes   **c)** about 50 minutes

(B) Listen to the conversation between Yoko and a clerk at a tourist information center and choose the best answer for each question.

Q4. About how much does it cost to get to downtown San Francisco by shuttle bus?

    a) $10   **b)** $20   **c)** $25

Q5. How did Yoko decide to get to her destination?

    a) by taxi   **b)** by bus   **c)** by train

> destination「目的地」

3 Dictation

CD 1-26, 27

Fill in the blanks while listening to the dialogs.

> **A. Dialog One**

Hiroshi: Hi. Could you tell me how to get (¹   )?

  Clerk: You can take BART, a bus, or a taxi. I recommend that you take BART.

Hiroshi: What's BART?

  Clerk: Oh, that's the abbreviation for Bay Area (²   ) (³   ).
      It's a fast train system serving the San Francisco Bay Area.

Hiroshi: I see. How (⁴   ) does it run?

  Clerk: It runs (⁵   ) 15 to 20 minutes.

Hiroshi: Does it stop near the, uh, Holiday Inn Express San Francisco Union Square?

  Clerk: Holiday Inn? At Union Square? Let me check [*Looking at the computer terminal*]. Yes, it's very close. You can walk there (⁶   ) a few minutes from Powell Station.

Hiroshi: Excuse me? What's the name of the station again?

  Clerk: Powell Station.

Hiroshi: Thanks. And how long does it (⁷   ) to get there?

  Clerk: Somewhere around (⁸   ) minutes.

14

UNIT 3 Getting to a Hotel

Hiroshi: OK. Where can I (⁹   ) the train?
Clerk: Just follow the signage. It's in the International Terminal, Boarding Area G.
Hiroshi: OK. I will. Thanks a lot.

B. Dialog Two

Yoko: Excuse me. Where can I catch a shuttle bus to downtown San Francisco?
Clerk: Just go outside the International Terminal. You can catch the shuttle there.
Yoko: Does it take long to get there?
Clerk: Well, it all (¹⁰   ) on the traffic, but it usually takes about (¹¹   ) minutes.
Yoko: I see. Do you know how much the (¹²   ) is?
Clerk: It shouldn't be so expensive. Around (¹³   ) dollars.
Yoko: Oh, that's a bit more expensive than I thought.
Clerk: Why don't you take BART? It should be less than (¹⁴   ) dollars.
Yoko: Excellent. I'll take your (¹⁵   ). Thanks.

4 Related Dialogs   CD 1-28, 29, 30

Listen to the three dialogs and choose the best answer for each question.

Dialog One

Question: **What form of transportation will she probably take?**
   a. taxi   b. bus   c. subway

| packed「混雑している」 take one's words for it「人の言うことを信じる」

Dialog Two

Question: **What time does this conversation take place?**
   a. 10:40   b. 10:45   c. 10:50

| bus schedule「バスの時刻表」

Dialog Three

Question: **About how long will it take to get to the California Hotel?**
   a. 15 minutes   b. 20 minutes   c. 25 minutes

15

5 Useful Expressions

 1-31

Listen and write the sentences.

1. ....
2. ....
3. ....
4. ....

6 Substitution Drills

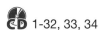 1-32, 33, 34

Complete the substitution drill in the following way.

(1) How often does <u>the subway</u> <u>run</u>?

> **Example:** the shuttle – run to the airport
> ➡ How often does the shuttle run to the airport?

a) the shuttle – run to the airport
b) the express – leave for the downtown area
c) the bus – run from the hotel to the aquarium

| aquarium 「水族館」

(2) I wouldn't <u>take a local train</u> if I were you.

> **Example:** go and see that movie
> ➡ I wouldn't go and see that movie if I were you.

a) go and see that movie
b) ask him for assistance
c) choose such an awful restaurant

| awful 「ひどい」

| UNIT 3 | Getting to a Hotel |

(3) Where can I catch a <u>shuttle bus</u> to <u>downtown San Francisco?</u>

> **Example:** train – downtown Boston
> ➡ Where can I catch a train to downtown Boston?

a) train – downtown Boston

b) taxi – the airport

c) bus – the shopping mall

7 Translation

Put the following Japanese sentences into English.

1. 地下鉄はどれくらいの間隔で運行していますか。

_____

2. ニューヨークの中心街までタクシーだといくらくらいかかりますか。

_____

3. 私だったら、各駅停車 (local train) には乗りませんよ。

_____

4. 空港行きのバスは 20 分おきに来ます。

_____

5. 道路状況にもよりますが、大体 20 〜 30 分くらいで着きます。

_____

17

8 Reading for Information

Read the following BART information and answer the questions below.

The quickest, easiest and cheapest method of getting to San Francisco and traveling around the Bay Area is BART. Trains arrive at the International Terminal of San Francisco Airport (SFO) every 15 minutes. A one-way ticket to downtown San Francisco, just a 30-minute ride away, costs $9.65. The Trip Planner will help find fares from SFO to any station.

To/from Downtown San Francisco

The Antioch train will take you to one of four downtown San Francisco stations that are an easy walk or short taxi ride to many San Francisco hotels. Below are the four downtown stations:

- **Montgomery Street** — Easy access to the Financial District and Moscone North/South. Use the Market/3rd Street exit for Moscone Center, Westin, The Palace and Financial District and South of Market (SOMA) hotels.
- **Powell Street** — The Hallidie Plaza exit provides access to the Intercontinental, Parc55, Hilton, and Union Square hotels. The 4th Street exit takes you to the Marriott and Moscone West.
- **Embarcadero** — Get off here for the Lower Financial District, Hyatt Regency and taxis to hotels on Fisherman's Wharf. The Drumm Street exit will take you right to the main entrance of the Hyatt.
- **Civic Center** — Get off here for Upper Market, Van Ness, the Castro and Civic Center districts. Take the Market/7th Street exit for the Proper Hotel.

SFO = San Francisco International Airport 国際航空輸送協会（IATA）が使用している3文字の空港コード

1. How often does the train come to SFO and how long does it take to get to downtown San Francisco?
2. How much do two one-way tickets to downtown San Francisco cost?
3. To get to the Marriott hotel, at which station should you get off? Which exit should you use?
4. Which is probably the most convenient station to get to Fisherman's Wharf?

UNIT 4
Checking into a Hotel

1 Pre-Listening Exercise

Guess what these words mean and match the appropriate meaning given in Japanese.

- ☐ a. reservation
- ☐ b. online
- ☐ c. enter
- ☐ d. PIN (Personal Identification Number)
- ☐ e. a copy of ~
- ☐ f. help yourself
- ☐ g. in-room Wi-Fi
- ☐ h. chest of drawers
- ☐ i. hotel directory
- ☐ j. include
- ☐ k. instructions on ~

---
1. ホテルの施設・サービスの説明書   2. ～を1部   3. 含む   4. 整理だんす
5. オンライン（インターネット）で   6. ～の指示；～の取扱説明書
7. ～を勝手（自由）に使う（取る）   8. 予約   9. 入力する   10. 暗証番号
11. 室内のWi-Fi（ワイファイ）

---

2 Comprehension Questions

 1-35, 36

(A) Listen to the conversation at the hotel and choose the best answer for each question.

Q1. How many nights will she be staying in this hotel?

    a) one night   **b)** two nights   **c)** three nights

Q2. Which of the following rooms will she be most likely to stay in?

    a) a single facing the sea

    b) a twin with a city view

    c) a single on the 10th floor

Q3. Which of the following questions did the guest ask the front desk clerk?
  a) room number and PIN
  b) PIN and breakfast hours
  c) breakfast hours and the availability of newspaper

(B) **Listen to the conversation between Yoko and the bellhop and choose the best answer for each question.**

Q4. How many pieces of baggage does she have?
  a) one   b) two   c) three

Q5. What did the bellhop tell the guest?
  a) the location of the hotel directory
  b) the location of the chest of drawers
  c) the location of the Wi-Fi hot spots

 **3 Dictation** 1-37, 38

Fill in the blanks while listening to the dialogs.

A. Checking in

Clerk: Good afternoon, ma'am. Welcome to the Intercontinental Hotel.
Yoko: Good afternoon. My name's Yoko Iwai. I made a reservation
        (¹   ) for two nights.
Clerk: Let me check. Just a (²   ). Of course, Ms. Iwai. A single for two
        (³   ), right?
Yoko: That's correct. Could I have a room with a nice (⁴   ) of the
        ocean?
Clerk: We have one single on the
        (⁵   ) floor. Is that OK?
Yoko: Fine.
Clerk: Could I have your credit card, please?
Yoko: Yes, here you (⁶   ).
Clerk: OK. Please (⁷   ) your PIN.
        [*She enters her PIN*] .... Thank you. You're in Room 1209.
Yoko: What time's breakfast?
Clerk: Breakfast is (⁸   ) 7:00 and 10:00 in the lounge.

UNIT 4 Checking into a Hotel

Yoko: OK. And could I have a (⁹   ) of today's paper?

Clerk: They're on the table over there. Help yourself.

B. Showing to the Room

Clerk: Is that all your baggage, ma'am?

Yoko: Yes, these two (¹⁰   ).

Clerk: Let me show you to your room. This way to
        the elevator. Please (¹¹   ) me.
        … [in the room]
        Where should I put your bags?

Yoko: Over there, (¹²   ) to the chest of
        drawers, thanks.

Clerk: Is there anything (¹³   ) I can do?

Yoko: Yes, could you tell me how to (¹⁴   ) to the in-room Wi-Fi?

Clerk: There's a hotel directory on the desk. That should (¹⁵   ) the
        instructions on how to connect to the in-room Wi-Fi.

Yoko: OK. Thanks.

Clerk: Enjoy your stay.

4 Related Dialogs

CD 1-39, 40, 41

Listen to the three dialogs and choose the best answer for each question.

Dialog One

Question: **What time does this conversation take place?**

   a. 1:30 p.m.   **b.** 2:00 p.m.   **c.** 2:30 p.m.

Dialog Two

Question: **What does she ask him to do?**

   a. take a walk and check out this area   **b.** carry her baggage to her room

   c. store her baggage

   ▌ look after「注意を払う；気を配る」

Dialog Three

Question: **What's the guest looking for?**

   a. information on the in-room Wi-Fi   **b.** information in the desk drawer

   c. information on her laptop

21

5 Useful Expressions

 1-42

Listen and write the sentences.

1. ....

2. ....

3. ....

4. ....

6 Substitution Drills

 1-43, 44, 45

Complete the substitution drill in the following way.

(1) I made a reservation <u>online</u> <u>for two nights</u>.

> **Example:** via Expedia – for a week
> ➡ I made a reservation via Expedia for a week.

a) via Expedia – for a week
b) through JTB – for three nights
c) for two twins – for tonight

| via「〜を介して」

(2) Could I have <u>a room</u> <u>with a nice view of the ocean</u>?

> **Example:** two singles – with a view of the city
> ➡ Could I have two singles with a view of the city?

a) two singles – with a view of the city
b) a twin – with a mountain view
c) a suite – on the upper floor

UNIT 4 Checking into a Hotel

(3) I want to <u>go for a walk</u> and <u>check out the area</u>.

> **Example:** take a walk – explore this area
>
> ➡ I want to take a walk and explore this area.

a) take a walk – explore this area

b) lie down – take a nap for a while

c) take a rest – relax for an hour or so

explore「探検（＝散策）する」

🌐 7 Translation

Put the following Japanese sentences into English.

1. インターネットで5泊の予約をしました。

_____

2. 私の部屋は上階にしてもらえますか。

_____

3. 部屋のWi-Fi（ワイファイ）の接続方法を教えてください。

_____

4. チェックイン・タイムまで、このスーツケースを預かってください。

_____

🌐 8 Reading for Information

Read the following hotel information and answer the questions.

Q1. Which of the following statements is true?

  a. You can check in at 2 p.m. and check out at 1 p.m.

  b. You can check in at 4 p.m. and check out at 10 a.m.

  c. You can check in at 8 p.m. and check out at 2 p.m.

  d. You can check in at 10 a.m. and check out at noon.

Q2. Which of the following combinations do you need when you check in to this hotel?

  a. a credit card and a passport

  b. cash and a reservation slip

  c. a return ticket and a passport

  d. a credit card and a reservation slip

23

Q3. **Which of the following statements is true?**

    a. This hotel has well over 180 rooms and 12 floors.

    b. An extra bed is available for less than 26 dollars.

    c. Two 19-year-olds can stay free with a parent.

    d. Transportation to the airport is available for hotel guests for less than 20 dollars.

Centrally Located San Francisco Hotel
Complimentary buffet-style breakfast and free Wi-Fi

Size

- 156 rooms on 8 floors

Arriving/leaving

- Check-in time is 2:00 PM-midnight /Check-out time is 12:00 noon (Late checkout possible by special arrangement)

Check-in requirements

- Credit card (for deposit) and official government-issued photo ID must be shown

Traveling with others

- Up to 2 children (18 years old and younger) may stay free of charge provided they occupy the parent or guardian's room. However, they must use the bedding provided and may not be eligible for free breakfast
- Rollaway beds are available at a cost of USD35.00 per night
- We do not accept pets, but service animals are welcome

Internet

- Free Wi-Fi in public areas and guest rooms

Transportation

- Airport shuttle runs every hour on the hour around the clock. Fare is USD18.00 per person (one-way)

Parking

- Self-parking for USD28.00 per night (availability limited)
- Parking for larger vehicles (RV/bus/truck, etc.) available at extra charge

Other information

- Smoking is prohibited in all rooms and public areas

---

be eligible for~「～の資格がある」 rollaway bed キャスター付きの折り畳み式ベッド
service animal「介助動物」身体障害者の日常生活を支援する訓練を受けた動物 one-way「片道」
RV = Recreational Vehicle

UNIT 5
Checking in without a Reservation

1 Pre-Listening Exercise

Guess what these words mean and match the appropriate meaning given in Japanese.

- ☐ a. a twin (room)
- ☐ b. service charge
- ☐ c. accept
- ☐ d. available
- ☐ e. fill out
- ☐ f. fully booked
- ☐ g. extend
- ☐ h. a couple of blocks away
- ☐ i. within walking distance

> 1. 予約で満室である　2. ツインルーム　3.（用紙などに）記入する
> 4. 徒歩圏に（ある）　5. 2ブロック離れた所に　6.（クレジットカードなどを）受け付ける
> 7. サービス料　8. 延長する　9. 空いている；利用できる

2 Comprehension Questions

 1-46

Listen to the dialog at the hotel and choose the best answer for each question.

Q1. What rooms are fully booked?
   a) singles with a mountain view
   b) twins with a city view
   c) singles with a city view

Q2. Which of the following rooms has Hiroshi decided to stay in?
   a) a single with a mountain view
   b) a twin with a city view
   c) a single with a city view

Q3. If he checks out at 2 p.m., how much will his payment for the room be?
   a) $123   b) $148   c) $210

25

Q4. Which of the following statements is true?

    a) The twins with a mountain view are fully booked.

    b) The usual check-out time is noon, but it can be extended until 3 p.m.

    c) Some restaurants are within walking distance from the hotel.

3 Dictation

CD 1-47

Fill in the blanks while listening to the dialogs.

Clerk: Good afternoon, sir. How can I help you?

Hiroshi: Hi. I need a room for tonight.

Clerk: Do you have a reservation?

Hiroshi: No, I don't. Could you check the (¹   )?

Clerk: All right. Would you like a single for (²   )?

Hiroshi: Yes. I want a room (³   ) a mountain view.

Clerk: I'm afraid all the singles with a mountain view are (⁴   ). There are some twins available, though.

Hiroshi: What's the (⁵   ) for the twin?

Clerk: It's (⁶   ) dollars including service charge.

Hiroshi: Do you have a single without a mountain view?

Clerk: Yes, we have a single with a city view available at (⁷   ) dollars.

Hiroshi: OK. I'll take that one.

Clerk: All right. Could you (⁸   ) out this registration card, please?

Hiroshi: Do you (⁹   ) Mastercard?

Clerk: Certainly. ... OK, your room is 1025.

Hiroshi: Thank you. ... What time do I have to check out tomorrow?

Clerk: Our normal check-out time is 11 o'clock, but you can (¹⁰   ) it to 3 p.m. for a (¹¹   )-dollar charge.

Hiroshi: I see. ... By the way, is there a restaurant in this hotel?

Clerk: No, but there are several fine restaurants just a couple of blocks (¹²   ). Just turn right out of the hotel.

Hiroshi: Good. Thanks a lot.

UNIT 5 | Checking in without a Reservation

4 Related Dialogs

 1-48, 49, 50

Listen to the three dialogs and choose the best answer for each question.

Dialog One

Question: **Which of the following statements is true?**

   a. She flew in from Phoenix, Arizona.

   b. She thinks the hotel rate is reasonable.

   c. She doesn't have a reservation.

> connecting flight「乗り継ぎ便」 stay overnight「一泊する」 full breakfast「卵料理にハム、ベーコンなどの肉類が付いた朝食」

Dialog Two

Question: **Which of the following statements is true?**

   a. She wants to reserve a single for August 13.

   b. The rate for a twin is $165.   c. Breakfast is served at an extra cost.

> buffet-style「バイキング（セルフサービスで食べ放題）形式の」

Dialog Three

Question: **Which of the following statements is true?**

   a. He wants to change the dates of his reservation.

   b. He wants to have two singles instead of a twin.

   c. He wants to change two twins to two singles.

5 Useful Expressions

 1-51

Listen and write the sentences.

1. ....

2. ....

3. ....

4. ....

6 Substitution Drills

 1-52, 53, 54

Complete the substitution drill in the following way.

(1) I need <u>a room for this evening</u>.

> **Example:** two singles for tonight
> ➡ I need two singles for tonight.

a) two singles for tonight
b) a twin for tomorrow
c) a suite for October 21

(2) I'm afraid <u>all the singles with a mountain view</u> are <u>reserved</u>.

> **Example:** our twins – all reserved
> ➡ I'm afraid our twins are all reserved.

a) our twins – all reserved
b) our singles with an ocean view – fully booked
c) all of our doubles – booked for that night

(3) I'd like to <u>book a twin for tonight</u>.

> **Example:** I want – book two singles for tomorrow night
> ➡ I want to book two singles for tomorrow night.

a) I want – book two singles for tomorrow night
b) I need – reserve a suite for November 12
c) I have – make a reservation for two twins for May 27 and 28

7 Translation

Put the following Japanese sentences into English.

1. シングルルームの料金はいくらですか。

2. アメリカンエクスプレス（American Express）は使えますか。

3. 2月18日と19日のツインルームを1部屋予約したい。

UNIT 5 Checking in without a Reservation

4. 明日のシングルルームは空いていますか。

---

8 Reading for Information

Read the following hotel advertisement and answer the questions.

Excelsior San Francisco International Airport

The Excelsior is a non-smoking hotel located just minutes from SFO and a BART station offering free continental breakfast.

It is located in a scenic spot near San Francisco and adjacent to the airport. There are a lot of advantages to being here in the heart of the Bay Area. You can find a wealth of restaurants, bars, and shops just a short walk away. Go just a little bit further and you'll be at the world-renowned Golden Gate Bridge, Fisherman's Wharf, and Pier 39. Go on a wine-tasting tour of Napa Valley or enjoy a Giants game at AT&T Park. There's no limit to your options!

Our hotel offers a complimentary daily breakfast and airport shuttle service. What's more, our friendly staff is on duty 24 hours a day to help in whatever way you want.

Our beautifully equipped rooms provide a comfortable space to sleep and relax. In addition, they offer a full range of modern amenities, and Dish Network allows you to access more than 100 high-definition TV channels for your viewing pleasure. Call to learn about all of our features and book your room at the Excelsior!

Featured Amenities
- Free Continental Breakfast
- Business Center
- Easy Access to Area Attractions
- Early Check-in Available (with small fee and based on availability)
- Refrigerator & Microwave
- Free Wi-Fi
- Free Shuttle to Airport & BART Station

continental beakfast パンと飲み物だけの朝食　in the heart of~「～の中心に」　complimentary「無料の」　equipped room「設備が整った客室」　amenities「アメニティー（生活を便利・快適にするもの）」　Dish Network「ディッシュ・ネットワーク」米国の衛星放送サービス　feature ~「～を呼び物・目玉にする」

29

Question: **Put T if the statement is true and F if it is not true.**

1. _____ This hotel offers free breakfast.

2. _____ Free Internet access is available to hotel guests.

3. _____ This hotel provides guests with free transportation to SFO.

4. _____ There is no restaurant within walking distance from the hotel.

5. _____ The Golden Gate Bridge and AT&T Park are within walking distance.

6. _____ The hotel staff is available around the clock.

7. _____ Shopping areas are probably nearby so you can walk there.

8. _____ You may check into this hotel earlier than the regular check-in time for a fee.

UNIT 6
At a Restaurant

1 Pre-Listening Exercise

Guess what these words mean and match the appropriate meaning given in Japanese.

- ☐ a. party
- ☐ b. server
- ☐ c. I'll be back in a moment.
- ☐ d. sparkling water
- ☐ e. house wine
- ☐ f. broiled
- ☐ g. platter
- ☐ h. fillet of sole
- ☐ i. stuffed clam
- ☐ j. come with ~
- ☐ k. Melba toast
- ☐ l. medium rare

> 1. シタビラメの骨なし切り身 2. ～を伴う；～が付いている 3. グループ、一行
> 4. かりかりに焼いた薄いトースト 5. 肉や野菜などで詰めものをして、オーブン焼きしたハマグリ 6. ミディアムとレアの中間の焼き方 7. 炭酸水 8. 盛り合わせの大皿料理
> 9. 給仕人（ウェイター，ウェイトレス） 10. 直火（放射熱）で焼いた
> 11. すぐに戻ります。   12. レストラン独自の手頃な価格のワイン

2 Comprehension Questions

 2-02, 03

(A) Listen to the conversation at a restaurant and choose the best answer for each question.

Q1. How many people are there in Yoko's group?
   a) one   b) two   c) three

Q2. What's Yoko's order?
   a) a steak sandwich and a glass of tomato juice
   b) a chickenburger and a glass of tomato juice
   c) a steak sandwich and a glass of iced tea

31

(B) **Listen to the conversation at a restaurant and choose the best answer for each question.**

Q3. What's Hiroshi's order?

   a) a glass of sparkling water, Caesar salad, and Broiled Captain's Platter
   b) a glass of house wine, chef's salad, and Broiled Captain's Platter
   c) a glass of house wine, Caesar salad, and New York steak

Q4. What dressing does Yoko want on her salad?

   a) Caesar   b) French   c) Italian

3 Dictation

 2-04, 05

Fill in the blanks while listening to the dialogs.

A. Ordering Lunch

Staff: Hi. How many are in your party?
Yoko: (¹   ) of us.
Staff: Come this way. … Is this table all right?
Yoko: Can we have a table (²   ) the window? We want to enjoy the (³   ) of the ocean.
Staff: Certainly. … How about this table? Is it OK with you?
Yoko: Yes. This is just fine.
Server: Okay. Here's the menu. I'll be back (⁴   ) a moment to take your order.
[*The server comes back to the table.*]
Can I (⁵   ) your order now?
Yoko: (⁶   ) have a steak sandwich.
Server: Anything to drink?
Yoko: (⁷   ) juice.
Server: Okay, and for you?
Hiroshi: I'd like a chickenburger and a glass of iced tea.
Server: Okay. Anything else?
Hiroshi: No, that's all.

B. Ordering Dinner

Server: Hi, my name is Cathy, and I'm your (⁸   ) tonight. How are you this evening?

UNIT 6 | At a Restaurant

Yoko: Fine, thanks.
Server: Would you like some drinks?
Yoko: I'll have a glass of (⁹   ) (¹⁰   ).
Server: And for you, sir?
Hiroshi: I'll have a glass of house wine — white, please.
Server: Okay. I'll be (¹¹   ) back with your drinks.
   Here's your water, … and wine. … Are you ready to order?
Hiroshi: Yes, I think so. Could you tell me what Broiled Captain's Platter is?
Server: Oh, it's a (¹²   ) of broiled salmon, fillet of sole, and stuffed clams.
Hiroshi: That (¹³   ) delicious. I'll have that. And I'd like the chef's salad.
Server: What kind of (¹⁴   ) would you like? We have Caesar, French, Italian, and Thousand Island.
Hiroshi: French, please.
Server: Anything else?
Hiroshi: No, that's all.
Server: Okay. And for you, ma'am?
Yoko: I'll have the New York steak and the house salad. Does the salad (¹⁵   ) with bread?
Server: Yes, it comes with Melba toast.
Yoko: I see.
Server: How would you (¹⁶   ) your steak?
Yoko: Medium rare. And I'd like Italian dressing on my salad.
Server: Okay. Anything else?
Yoko: No, that's all.
Server: Thank you. I'll be right back (¹⁷   ) your order.

4 Related Dialogs

 2-06, 07, 08

Listen to the three dialogs and choose the best answer for each question.

Dialog One

Question: **Which of the following statements is true?**
   a. He wants to reserve a table for tomorrow at 7:15.
   b. He wants to book a table for tomorrow at a quarter to seven.
   c. He is willing to wait for a few minutes until the table is ready.

33

Dialog Two

Question: **What is the woman most likely to say next?**

    a. I'd like them sunny-side up.   **b.** I'd like two fresh eggs.

    c. I'll have three slices of bacon, please.

> sunny-side up「目玉焼き（半熟片面焼き）」

Dialog Three

Question: **Which of the following statements is true?**

    a. The man wants some pie for dessert.

    b. The woman wants some ice cream for dessert.

    c. Neither of them wants dessert.

> full「おなかがいっぱいで」　have no room for ~「~のための余裕がない」　sundae「サンデー（シロップやナッツなどをトッピングしたアイスクリーム）」　refill「お代わり」

5 Useful Expressions

Listen and write the sentences.

1. ....

2. ....

3. ....

4. ....

6 Substitution Drills

Complete the substitution drill in the following way.

(1) I'll have the <u>New York Steak</u> and <u>the house salad</u>.

> **Example:** lobster – the Caesar salad
> ➡ I'll have the lobster and the Caesar salad.

UNIT 6　At a Restaurant

a) lobster – the Caesar salad

b) chicken – a bowl of clam chowder

c) scallops – the tossed salad

scallop「ホタテ」　tossed salad「ボウルに野菜とドレッシングを入れて軽く混ぜ合わせたサラダ」

(2) It's a combination of <u>broiled salmon, fillet of sole</u>, and <u>stuffed clams</u>.

> **Example:** cheese, vegetables – meat
>
> ➡ It's a combination of cheese, vegetables, and meat.

a) cheese, vegetables – meat

b) octopus, shrimp – scallops

c) shrimp, chicken – pork

octopus「タコ」

(3) I'd like to <u>reserve a table</u> for <u>three people for tomorrow</u>.

> **Example:** book a table – five people for this evening
>
> ➡ I'd like to book a table for five people for this evening.

a) book a table – five people for this evening

b) make a reservation – two people for tonight

c) make a booking – six people for tomorrow

7 Translation

Put the following Japanese sentences into English.

1. 何名様ですか。

_____

2. The antipasto platter は、チーズと野菜と肉の盛り合わせ料理です。

_____

3. サラダのドレッシングは何になさいますか。

_____

4. ステーキの焼き方はどうなさいますか。

_____

5. すぐにコーヒーをお持ちいたします。

_____

35

🌐 8 Vocabulary

Here are some words often used in restaurants. Match the following English vocabulary items with the Japanese translations provided below.

1. a la carte	2. appetizer	3. bake
4. beverage	5. boil	6. broil
7. brunch	8. buffet	9. chop
10. clam	11. crab	12. deep-fry
13. dip	14. entree	15. flounder
16. stir-fry	17. grill	18. leftovers
19. lobster	20. mash	21. mayonnaise
22. nutritious	23. oyster	24. scallop
25. salmon	26. season	27. simmer
28. shrimp	29. sprinkle	30. steam
31. turkey	32. squid	33. trout
34. tuna	35. veal	36. roast

飲み物	カキ	ホタテ
エビ	伊勢エビ	ハマグリ
サケ	ヒラメ	イカ
カニ	主菜（メインディッシュ）	前菜
マグロ	マス	バイキング
朝食兼用昼食	一品料理	（包丁などで）細かく切る
味付けする	食べ残し	マヨネーズ
栄養価の高い	子牛の肉	弱火でことこと煮る
蒸す	つぶす	たっぷりの油で揚げる
振りかける	（液体などに）ちょっとつける・浸す	ゆでる
網焼き・鉄板焼きにする	（パン、野菜などを）オーブンで焼く	直火で焼く
強火ですばやく炒める	七面鳥	（肉類を）オーブンで焼く

Taking the Subway

1 Pre-Listening Exercise

Guess what these words mean and match the appropriate meaning given in Japanese.

☐ **a.** American Museum of Natural History ☐ **b.** transfer ☐ **c.** stop
☐ **d.** I wonder ~ ☐ **e.** track ☐ **f.** fare ☐ **g.** vending machine

> 1. 運賃   2. 線路，プラットフォーム   3. アメリカ自然史博物館   4. 自動販売機
> 5. ~を知りたいと思う   6. 乗り換える   7. 停車駅

2 Comprehension Questions   CD 2-13

Listen to the conversation and choose the best answer for each question.

Q1. Which lines does Hiroshi have to take to get to the American Museum of Natural History?
   a) A Line towards 140th Street
   b) B Line towards 145th Street
   c) C Line towards 150th Street

Q2. How many stops is it to the museum?
   a) six   b) seven   c) eight

Q3. How much is the fare?
   a) $2.50   b) $3.00   c) $3.50

37

Q4. If Hiroshi takes the 2:25 train, what time does he expect to arrive at the Museum?

    a) 2:35   **b)** 2:40   **c)** 2.45

3 Dictation

CD 2-14, 15

Fill in the blanks while listening to the conversation.

> **A. At a Hotel**

Hiroshi: Excuse me. Could you tell me (¹   ) to get to the American Museum of Natural History from here?

Hotel Clerk: You can (²   ) the subway. It's probably the (³   ).

Hiroshi: What's the (⁴   ) subway station?

Hotel Clerk: 34th Street-Herald Square. It's about a 5-minute (⁵   ) from here.

        [*At 34th Street-Herald Square*]

Hiroshi: Which (⁶   ) should I take to get to the American Museum of Natural History?

Station Worker A: Take the B Line towards 145th Street.

Hiroshi: Do I have to (⁷   ) somewhere?

Station Worker A: No, the train will take you (⁸   ) to the museum.

Hiroshi: How many (⁹   ) is it?

Station Worker A: It's the (¹⁰   ) stop from here.

Hiroshi: I wonder how long it'll take.

Station Worker A: It'll take about (¹¹   ) minutes.

Hiroshi: What's the (¹²   )?

Station Worker A: (¹³   ) dollars. You can buy a ticket at the (¹⁴   ) machine over there.

Hiroshi: Thank you.

UNIT 7　Taking the Subway

B. On the platform

Hiroshi: Excuse me. What track does the train to the American Museum of Natural History (¹⁵   ) from?

Station Worker B: From the (¹⁶   ) track.

Hiroshi: When does the next train (¹⁷   )?

Station Worker B: It should be arriving (¹⁸   ) five minutes.

Hiroshi: Thanks. You've been very helpful.

4 Related Dialogs

 2-16, 17, 18

Listen to the three dialogs and choose the best answer for each question.

Dialog One

Question: **Where is the train arriving?**

  a. London　　**b.** platform 4　　**c.** in two minutes

Dialog Two

Question: **What time does this conversation take place?**

  a. 10:40　　**b.** 10:42　　**c.** 10:45

| due「到着する予定である」　train schedule「時刻表」

Dialog Three

Question: **You just missed the 10:45 train. When is the next train due?**

  a. 11:05　　**b.** 11:15　　**c.** 11:25

5 Useful Expressions

 2-19

Listen and write the sentences.

1. ......
2. ......
3. ......
4. ......

6 Substitution Drills

 2-20, 21, 22

Complete the substitution drill in the following way.

(1) Which line <u>should I</u> take to get to <u>the American Museum of Natural History</u>?

> **Example:** do I – the Empire State Building
> ➡ Which line do I take to get to the Empire State Building?

a) do I – the Empire State Building

b) are we supposed to – Times Square

c) do I need to – the Metropolitan Museum of Art

(2) <u>What track</u> does <u>the train to the museum</u> leave from?

> **Example:** Which track – the train for Shizuoka
> ➡ Which track does the train for Shizuoka leave from?

a) Which track – the train for Shizuoka

b) Which platform – the train to Shinjuku

c) Where – the bus to the airport

UNIT 7 Taking the Subway

(3) **You have to transfer at <u>Grand Central Terminal</u> to get to <u>Times Square</u>.**

> **Example:** Shinjuku – Tokyo
> ➡ You have to transfer at Shinjuku to get to Tokyo.

a) Shinjuku – Tokyo

b) Akihabara – Yotsuya

c) Namba – Umeda

🌐 7 Translation

Put the following Japanese sentences into English.

1. 次の東京行きの列車は何時に到着しますか。

_____

2. 品川から横浜はいくつ目の駅ですか。

_____

3. ここから新宿へ行くにはどうしたらいいですか。

_____

4. 秋葉原で山手線か京浜東北線に乗り換えてください。

_____

5. その列車に乗れば神戸までは乗り換えなしで行けます。

_____

41

8 Reading for Information

Look at the Los Angeles Metro map and answer the questions in English.

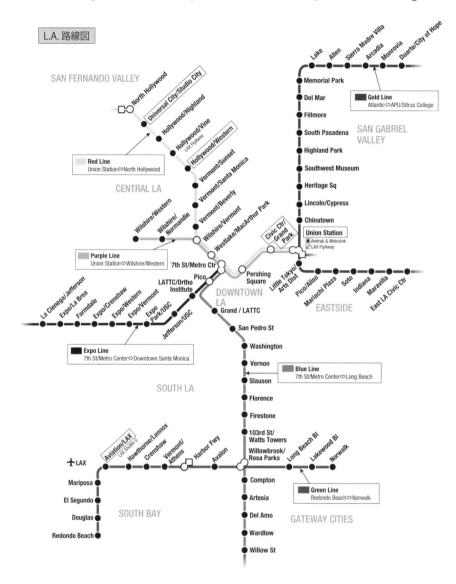

1. You are at Civic Center/Grand Park. How many stops is it to Universal City/Studio City?

2. Suppose you are at Hollywood/Western on the Red Line. How many times do you have to change trains to get to LAX Airport?

3. Explain how to get to Union Station from LAX Airport by filling in the blanks.
   Take the _____ Line to get to _____. Then transfer to the _____ Line.
   Get off at _____ and take the Red Line. Union Station is the _____ stop.

UNIT 8
At a Fast-Food Restaurant

1 Pre-Listening Exercise

Guess what these words mean and match the appropriate meaning given in Japanese.

- a. to go
- b. in a hurry
- c. French fries
- d. change
- e. Is that for here?
- f. turkey
- g. taste
- h. care for ~
- i. cashier
- j. on your way out

1. ~がほしい　2. レジ係　3. フライドポテト　4. こちらでお召し上がりですか。
5. 七面鳥　6. 味がする　7. 持ち帰り用の　8. お帰りの際に　9. お釣り
10. 急いで

2 Comprehension Questions

 2-23, 24

(A) Listen to the conversation at a fast-food restaurant and choose the best answer for each question.

Q1. What did Hiroshi order?

   a) a Bigburger, large French fries and a medium cola
   b) a double fishburger, medium French fries and a small cola
   c) a double fishburger, small French fries and a large cola

Q2. Which of the following best describes Yoko's order?

   a) a large pizza and a small cola to go
   b) a medium pizza and a small coffee for here
   c) a small pizza and a large coffee for here

43

(B) Listen to the dialog at a snack bar and choose the best answer for each question.

Q3. Why does Yoko want to have a turkey sandwich?

   a) because it's her favorite

   b) because she doesn't like the other sandwiches

   c) because it's new to her

Q4. What beverage did Yoko order?

   a) coffee   b) iced tea   c) Coke

3 Dictation

 2-25, 26

Fill in the blanks while listening to the dialogs.

A. At a Fast-Food Restaurant

Cashier: May I (¹   ) your order?

Hiroshi: Yes. I'd like a Bigburger and French fries to go, please.

Cashier: Sorry. The Bigburgers aren't (²   ) yet. It'll take about 10 minutes. Can you wait?

Hiroshi: No, I'm (³   ) a hurry. I'll have a double fishburger instead.

Cashier: Okay. What (⁴   ) fries would you like?

Hiroshi: Small would be fine.

Cashier: All right. Anything to drink?

Hiroshi: Oh, yes. I'd like a (⁵   ) cola.

Cashier: We only serve small or large.

Hiroshi: I'll have a large then.

Cashier: That's $6.50. And 50 cents is your (⁶   ). Thank you.

Cashier: Next, please.

Yoko: I'd like a medium pizza and a small (⁷   ).

Cashier: Is that for here or (⁸   ) go?

Yoko: For here.

Cashier: That's $4.45.

Yoko: Here you are.

Cashier: And $5.55 is your change.

UNIT 8　At a Fast-Food Restaurant

B. At a Snack Bar

Server: Are you (⁹　　　　) to order?

Yoko: Yes. I'd like a sandwich. What kind do you have?

Server: Well, we (¹⁰　　　　) ham, cheese, chicken, turkey...

Yoko: I've (¹¹　　　　) had a turkey sandwich. I'll try one and see how it (¹²　　　　).

Server: Okay. Would you (¹³　　　　) for anything to drink with that?

Yoko: I'll have a glass of iced tea.

Server: Okay. I'll be (¹⁴　　　　) back. ... Here's your sandwich and coffee.

Yoko: I didn't order coffee. I (¹⁵　　　　) for iced tea.

Server: Oh, I'm sorry. I'll be right back with your tea. ... Here you are. Sorry about that.

Yoko: That's all right. Should I pay you now?

Server: Please pay the (¹⁶　　　　) on your way out.

4 Related Dialogs

CD 2-27, 28, 29

Listen to the three dialogs and choose the best answer for each question.

Dialog One

Question: **What is she most likely to say next?**

　　a. blue　　　b. expensive　　　c. vanilla

Dialog Two

Question: **What is his order?**

　　a. a cheeseburger and large French fries

　　b. two cheeseburgers and small French fries

　　c. two cheeseburgers, a small fried chicken and a cup of coffee

Dialog Three

Question: **What does she want for her hot dog?**

　　a. mustard and ketchup　　　　b. ketchup and onions

　　c. mustard and onions

45

5 Useful Expressions

 2-30

Listen and write the sentences.

1. ....
2. ....
3. ....
4. ....

6 Substitution Drills

 2-31, 32, 33

Complete the substitution drill in the following way.

(1) I'd like <u>a Bigburger and French fries</u> <u>to go</u>.

> **Example:** a double fishburger and a small Coke – for here
> ➡ I'd like a double fishburger and a small Coke for here.

a) a double fishburger and a small Coke – for here

b) two hamburgers and large fries – to go

c) a small fried chicken and a medium coffee – for here

(2) <u>The cheeseburgers</u> aren't ready yet. How about <u>a chickenburger</u>?

> **Example:** The double chickenburgers – a teriyaki burger
> ➡ The double chickenburgers aren't ready yet. How about a teriyaki burger?

a) The double chickenburgers – a teriyaki burger

b) The fishburgers – a double cheeseburger

c) The chicken nuggets – French fries

UNIT 8 At a Fast-Food Restaurant

(3) Would you <u>care for</u> <u>anything to drink</u>?

> **Example:** like – some dessert
> ➡ Would you like some dessert?

a) like – some dessert

b) care for – anything else

c) like – some more coffee

7 Translation

Put the following Japanese sentences into English.

1. ご注文はお決まりでしょうか。

   _____

2. フィッシュバーガーとコーラを持ち帰りでお願いします。

   _____

3. こちらでお召し上がりですか、それともお持ち帰りですか。

   _____

4. チーズバーガーはまだ用意できておりません。チキンバーガーではいかがでしょうか。

   _____

5. 私が注文したのはオレンジジュースで、コーヒーではありません。

   _____

8 Reading for Information

Read the following article on Wendy's and write T if the statement is true and F if it is not true.

1. _____ Dave Thomas established Wendy's in the State of Ohio in the 19th century.

2. _____ There are more than 6,000 Wendy's restaurants in the United States.

3. _____ American fast food restaurants normally offer hamburgers, fries, and salads.

4. _____ Wendy's was once famous for its uniquely shaped burgers.

5. _____ Jalapeno ghost pepper fries are spicy.

6. _____ Wendy's menu prices are the same in different areas of the United States.

7. _____ The quality of meals in Wendy's is high, and so are the prices.

8. _____ Unlike other fast food chains, Wendy's serves fresh meat.

47

Wendy's — established by Dave Thomas in 1969 in Columbus, Ohio — is an American fast-food chain popular all over the world. As of 2016, this gigantic fast-food chain has over 6,000 restaurants across the globe.

Wendy's menu is comparable to that of typical American hamburger shops like McDonald's and Burger King. It offers hamburgers, chicken sandwiches, French fries, as well as healthy options like salads and beverages, including its signature frozen dessert, Frosty. At one time, Wendy's was known for its square hamburgers and sandwiches, sea salt French fries, and the Frosty. Although the original idea of this restaurant chain is to offer old-fashioned food, Wendy's has successfully adjusted itself to the notion of modern food establishments.

Wendy's offers real comfort food. Everyone surely loves a 100-percent beef patty topped with melted cheese, onions, tomatoes on a bed of lettuce, and served in a soft bun. Wendy's burgers and its old-fashioned fries usually make a good combo. However, if you're feeling in the mood for something hot, why not try Wendy's jalapeno ghost pepper fries? They also offer baked potatoes that match their burger selections.

Wendy's menu prices may vary depending on which state you are in, but you will always be sure of getting high-quality, delicious meals at a reasonable price. What really distinguishes Wendy's from other fast-food chains is its dedication to freshness in its meats and other ingredients while still giving value for money. Most burger chains today use frozen meat patties, but Wendy's is committed to serving meats that are "always fresh and never frozen." And that may be part of the reason why people love this traditional fast-food chain.

comparable to ~「~に似ている」 signature「代表的・特徴的な」 comfort food 子供の頃を思い出すような、ほっこり癒され、幸福感を与える料理；ソウルフード patty ひき肉などを薄く平たくしたもの combo「(特にファストフードの店で) 料理の組み合わせ」 ingredient「材料」

UNIT 9
Hotel Services

1 Pre-Listening Exercise

Guess what these words mean and match the appropriate meaning given in Japanese.

☐ **a.** wonder if   ☐ **b.** actually   ☐ **c.** five minutes' drive
☐ **d.** feel like going out   ☐ **e.** in that case   ☐ **f.** That's an idea.
☐ **g.** laundry [lɔ́ːndri]   ☐ **h.** following day   ☐ **i.** slip   ☐ **j.** drop off

---
1. それはいいアイディアだ。　2. 翌日　3. 伝票　4. 洗濯物　5.（人・荷物を）降ろす　6.（〜かどうか）と思う　7. 外出したい気分である　8. 車で5分（の距離）　9. その場合には　10. 実は

---

2 Comprehension Questions

 2-34, 35

(A) Listen to the dialog at the hotel and choose the best answer for each question.

Q1. Which of the following orders is correct?

　a) seafood dinner and coffee

　b) seafood burger and iced tea

　c) seafood pasta and iced tea

Q2. Which of the following statements is correct?

　a) Adams Street is within walking distance.

　b) Room service is open until 11 p.m.

　c) Her room number is 1213.

(B) Listen to the dialog at the hotel and choose the best answer for each question.

Q3. What time does he expect to pick up the cleaning?

a) 7 a.m.   b) 10 a.m.   c) 5 p.m.

Q4. Which of the following statements is NOT true?

a) He has to fill in the laundry slip in order to use the cleaning service.

b) Items that need washing are supposed to be found in the closet.

c) The express cleaning is 20 percent more expensive than the regular service.

3 Dictation

 2-36, 37

Fill in the blanks while listening to the dialogs.

A. Ordering Room Service

Yoko: Hi, I just checked in and I'm wondering (¹   ) there's a restaurant in this hotel.

Clerk: I'm afraid there isn't one, but there are some restaurants on Adams Street.

Yoko: Is it within walking (²   )?

Clerk: No, it's about five minutes' (³   ).

Yoko: Actually, I don't feel like going out. I'm so tired.

Clerk: In that case, how about trying our room service? It's (⁴   ) till 11 p.m.

Yoko: That's an idea. I might do that. Thank you.

[Later Yoko makes a phone call to order room service.]

RS: Room Service, may I help you?

Yoko: Yes, I'd like to order the seafood (⁵   ).

RS: All right? Anything to drink?

Yoko: I want a glass of iced (⁶   ).

RS: Would you like some dessert?

Yoko: No thanks. That's all.

RS: All right. May I have your room number, please?

Yoko: (⁷   ).

RS: Thank you very much, ma'am. Your order will take about 20 minutes.

UNIT 9 Hotel Services

B. Asking for Laundry Service

Hiroshi: I'd like some clothes (⁸   ). Do you have a laundry service?

Clerk: Yes. If you bring your laundry before 10 a.m., it'll be done by (⁹   ) a.m. on the following day.

Hiroshi: That's too late. I have to leave before (¹⁰   ) tomorrow morning.

Clerk: We offer express service for an extra charge. You can get your laundry by (¹¹   ) p.m. on the same day.

Hiroshi: How much extra?

Clerk: Our express service costs you 20 (¹²   ) more than regular service.

Hiroshi: I see. I'll use the express service. What should I do?

Clerk: There's a laundry bag in the (¹³   ). Just put your items in, fill out the laundry slip, and (¹⁴   ) it off at the front desk.

Hiroshi: OK. Thanks a lot.

4 Related Dialogs

 2-38, 39, 40

Listen to the three dialogs and choose the best answer for each question.

Dialog One

Question: **At what time is the taxi arriving at the hotel?**

　　a. 10 a.m.　　b. 9:45 a.m.　　c. 10:15 a.m.

　　| Convention Center 「コンベンション・センター」展示会や会議などを行う施設

Dialog Two

Question: **What does he want to do at the business center?**

　　a. He wants to go to the second floor.
　　b. He wants to use Wi-Fi.
　　c. He wants to use a printer.

　　| business center インターネットに接続された PC、プリンター、コピー、ファクシミリなどのビジネスに必要な OA 機器を備えたホテルの施設で、小規模の会議が行われることもある。

Dialog Three

Question: **How long does it take to get to his destination?**

    a. 10 minutes   b. 15 minutes   c. 50 minutes

5 Useful Expressions

 2-41

Listen and write the sentences.

1. ....

2. ....

3. ....

4. ....

6 Substitution Drills

 2-42, 43, 44

Complete the substitution drill in the following way.

(1) I'm wondering if <u>there's a restaurant</u> in this hotel.

> **Example:** there's a fitness room
> ➡ I'm wondering if there's a fitness room in this hotel.

    a) there's a fitness room

    b) there's a dry-cleaning service

    c) there's free Internet access

(2) <u>Our express service</u> costs you <u>20 percent more</u>.

> **Example:** Flying first class – a lot of money
> ➡ Flying first class costs you a lot of money.

a) Flying first class – a lot of money

b) A new laptop – around $1,000

c) This service – nothing

(3) How can I get to the <u>metro station</u> from <u>here</u>?

> **Example:** art museum – the hotel
> ➡ How can I get to the art museum from the hotel?

a) art museum – the hotel

b) baseball stadium – the shopping mall

c) bank – the subway station

7 Translation

Put the following Japanese sentences into English.

1. このホテルにサウナ（sauna）はありますか。

_____

2. マジソン通り（Madison Street）にいくつか銀行があります。

_____

3. あまり遠くまで歩きたくありません。タクシーを呼んでいただけますか。

_____

4. そのホテルから中心街に（downtown）はどう行ったらいいですか。

_____

🌐 8 Vocabulary

Fill in the blanks with the words and phrases provided below.

1. Could you (   ) me up at 5:00 tomorrow morning?
   明日の朝、5:00に起こしてもらえますか。

2. I'd like to (   ) one more night.
   もう1泊滞在したいのですが。

3. I need a (   ) to the airport. Do you have a shuttle service?
   空港までの移動手段が必要です。シャトルサービスはありますか。

4. I need some U.S. dollars. Is (   ) an ATM near here?
   いくらかUSドルが必要です。近くにATMはありますか。

5. Could you (   ) any Chinese or Japanese restaurants nearby?
   近くにある中華料理店か日本料理店のお薦めを教えていただけますか。

6. I've (   ) myself out of the room.
   部屋から閉め出されてしまいました。

7. I want to have my suit (   ).
   スーツのクリーニングをお願いしたいのですが。

8. How can I (   ) to the fitness room?
   フィットネスルームへはどう行ったらいいですか。

9. One of my friends is (   ) in the elevator.
   友人の1人がエレベーターに閉じ込められました。

10. Could you (   ) someone up to my room to pick up my suitcases?
    スーツケースを取りに、誰かを私の部屋へよこしてもらえますか。

cleaned	get	locked	recommend	ride
send	stay	stuck	there	wake

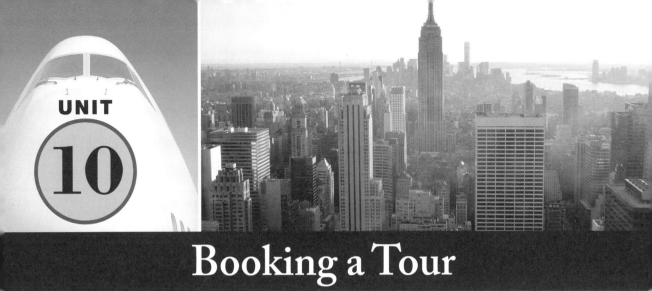

UNIT 10
Booking a Tour

1 Pre-Listening Exercise

Guess what these words mean and match the appropriate meaning given in Japanese.

☐ a. sightseeing tour   ☐ b. brochure   ☐ c. guided tour   ☐ d. landmark
☐ e. district   ☐ f. the Statue of Liberty   ☐ g. and much more
☐ h. involve ~   ☐ i. availability   ☐ j. One World Observatory
☐ k. admission fee   ☐ l. MetroCard   ☐ m. Fair enough.

> 1. 冊子，パンフレット 2. ワンワールド展望台 3. 入場料 4. 利用できる可能性
> 5. ～を伴う・含む 6. いいでしょう（同意するよ）。 7. NY市地下鉄・市バスを利用できるプリペイドカード 8. ガイド付きのツアー 9. 自由の女神 10. 地区
> 11. 目印，歴史的建造物 12. 観光ツアー 13. 他にもたくさんある

2 Comprehension Questions

 2-45

Listen to the dialog between Hiroshi and hotel clerk and choose the best answer for each question.

Q1. What kind of New York City tour is Hiroshi interested in?

　a) a full-day guided tour

　b) a half-day sightseeing tour

　c) a seven-hour walking tour

Q2. Which of the following landmark locations did the clerk NOT mention?

　a) the Broadway Theater district

　b) the Empire State Building

　c) Rockefeller Center

55

Q3. When and where does the tour end?

   a) It ends at the hotel where Hiroshi is staying at 9.

   b) It ends in downtown Manhattan at 3.

   c) It ends at the One World Observatory at 4.

Q4. What is NOT included in the price?

   a) a ticket to One World Observatory

   b) a ferry ticket

   c) a $10 MetroCard

3 Dictation

 2-46

Fill in the blanks while listening to the dialog.

[*At the Information/Concierge Desk*]

Hiroshi: Hi, I'm wondering if there's a (¹   ) tour of New York City.

Clerk: Yes, would you like a full-day tour or a (²   ) tour?

Hiroshi: A full-day tour.

Clerk: How about this small-group tour? [*showing a brochure*] This is one of the most popular city tours, and the price is pretty (³   ), too.

Hiroshi: Sounds interesting. Could you be more (⁴   )? What can I (⁵   ) from this tour?

Clerk: Well, this (⁶   ) tour covers many of the famous (⁷   ) locations and sites, such as Times Square, the Broadway Theater district, the Empire State Building, Grand Central Terminal, the Brooklyn Bridge, the (⁸   ) of Liberty, and much more. This is an excellent tour for first-time (⁹   ).

Hiroshi: That sounds like the tour I want. Is it a bus tour?

Clerk: No, you take a subway train and ferry. This tour (¹⁰   ) a lot of walking, too.

Hiroshi: Good. That's (¹¹   ) I need most, a lot of walking! How much is it?

Clerk: When do you plan to join the tour?

Hiroshi: Tomorrow.

UNIT 10   Booking a Tour

Clerk: Let me check the availability. … Yes, it's available for tomorrow, and the price is $109 for (^{12}).

Hiroshi: I see. When and (^{13}) does this tour start?

Clerk: Let's see. … It starts right in front of this hotel at 9 a.m. and (^{14}) at the One World Observatory in downtown Manhattan at around 4 p.m. It's a (^{15}) tour.

Hiroshi: Does the price (^{16}) everything? I mean, tax and admission (^{17})?

Clerk: An admission ticket to One World Observatory, a ferry ticket and tax are included, but you need a 10-dollar MetroCard to take the subway. Also, food and (^{18}) are not included.

Hiroshi: Okay, fair (^{19}). I'll take it. Could you make a reservation for me?

Clerk: Sure.

4 Related Dialogs

CD 2-47, 48, 49

Listen to the three dialogs and choose the best answer for each question.

Dialog One

Question: **When does the man expect to be back?**

   a. June 5   **b.** June 6   **c.** June 7

Dialog Two

Question: **Which of the following statements is true?**

   a. This tour crosses the Golden Gate Bridge.

   b. This tour involves four hours of free time in Yosemite National Park.

   c. This is a two-day tour from San Francisco to Yosemite National Park.

   sleep on~「～を一晩考える」

Dialog Three

Question: **Why did the clerk recommend that the visitor buy a seven-day pass?**

   a. The visitor is staying in New York for a week.

   b. The seven-day pass is the only type available.

   c. The seven-day pass may turn out to be less expensive.

   in the long run「結局は」

57

5 Useful Expressions

 2-50

Listen and write the sentences.

1. ....
2. ....
3. ....
4. ....

6 Substitution Drills

 2-51, 52, 53

Complete the substitution drill in the following way.

(1) I'm wondering if <u>there's a sightseeing tour</u> of <u>New York City</u>.

> **Example:** there's a half-day sightseeing tour – San Francisco
> ➡ I'm wondering if there's a half-day sightseeing tour of San Francisco.

  a) there's a half-day sightseeing tour – San Francisco
  b) there's a helicopter tour – Chicago
  c) there're many guided tours – Washington, D.C.

(2) This tour covers <u>many</u> of <u>the famous landmark locations and sites</u>.

> **Example:** a lot – scenic spots and historic sites
> ➡ This tour covers a lot of scenic spots and historic sites.

  a) a lot – scenic spots and historic sites
  b) two – UNESCO's world heritage sites
  c) some – the most amazing landscapes in California

scenic spots「景勝地」　historic site「旧跡, 史跡」　world heritage「世界遺産」　landscape「風景, 景観」

UNIT 10 Booking a Tour

(3) **This tour** involves a lot of walking.

> **Example:** consists of a scenic drive along the Pacific Ocean
> ➡ This tour consists of a scenic drive along the Pacific Ocean.

a) consists of a scenic drive along the Pacific Ocean

b) includes five miles of hiking

c) involves a 15-minute helicopter ride

7 Translation

Put the following Japanese sentences into English.

1. Washington, D.C. の市内ツアーはあるのでしょうか。

_____

2. このツアーには20分間のヘリコプター飛行が含まれ、それはニューヨークの息をのむような夜景（breathtaking night views of 〜）をあなたに提供してくれます。

_____

3. このツアーは、多くの景勝地やUNESCOの世界遺産をカバーしています。

_____

4. このツアーは何時ごろ、どこで終了しますか。

_____

8 Reading for Information

Read the following tour advertisement and write T if the statement is true and F if it is not true.

1. _____ This tour is a two-day round trip from New York City to Washington, D.C.

2. _____ The tour includes some of the admission fees to the sites, but not all of them.

3. _____ Free Internet access is available on the bus.

4. _____ The itinerary includes only a few opportunities for picture-taking.

5. _____ The tour takes you to the gravesite of John F. Kennedy.

6. _____ You will be seeing the Capitol Building.

7. _____ The itinerary includes a visit to one of the space museums.

8. _____ The famous attractions in Washington, D.C. are located near the National Mall.

59

Washington, D.C. One-Day Trip From New York City

This day trip from New York City to Washington, D.C. allows you to see the most famous sights of the nation's capital in just one day. As a bonus, all transportation and entrance fees are included. After traveling by van or bus to D.C., you'll get a panoramic sightseeing tour that takes in major landmarks such as the White House, the Washington Monument and the Lincoln Memorial. In addition, you will also visit Arlington National Cemetery and the Smithsonian National Air and Space Museum.

Highlights
- Full-day trip to Washington, D.C. from New York City
- Guided panoramic tour of Washington, D.C.
- Entertaining and expert commentary from your tour guide
- Air-conditioned deluxe van or bus
- Free Wi-Fi on the bus

Why People Choose This Tour

Some people don't have the time to take a full trip to Washington, D.C. and can only spare a day. If so, our compact, well-organized itinerary will help you make the most of your limited time in the nation's capital. With informative commentary and plenty of stops for photos, this tour would be a great addition to your New York City trip.

What to Expect

Our day trip begins with a drive south from New York City, passing through three states — New Jersey, Delaware and Maryland — before arriving in the capital. Your tour starts at Arlington National Cemetery, where you can visit the gravesite of President John F. Kennedy. Then we'll drive through the city center to see famous landmarks like the Capitol Building and the White House before visiting the National Air and Space Museum, which is part of the Smithsonian Institution. In conclusion, you'll have the chance to take memorable photos at some of D.C.'s most famous attractions, which are clustered around the National Mall — the Lincoln Memorial, the Washington Monument and the Korean War Veterans Memorial. Then we'll head back to NYC, where your day trip ends.

---

the Lincoln Memorial「リンカーン記念堂」 Arlington National Cemetery「アーリントン国立墓地」
the Smithsonian National Air and Space Museum「スミソニアン国立航空宇宙博物館」
spare a day「1日（の時間）を空ける」 the Capitol Building「連邦議会（国会）議事堂」
the National Mall ワシントン中心部の国立公園　the Korean War Veterans Memorial「朝鮮戦争戦没者慰霊碑」

UNIT 11
Health Care

1 Pre-Listening Exercise

Guess what these words mean and match the appropriate meaning given in Japanese.

☐ a. pharmacist ☐ b. heal ☐ c. crick ☐ d. sleep wrong ☐ e. patch
☐ f. eye drops ☐ g. irritated ☐ h. aisle [áil] ☐ i. work for ~
☐ j. hay fever ☐ k. allergy ☐ l. relief ☐ m. symptom ☐ n. sneeze
☐ o. suffer from ~ ☐ p. runny nose ☐ q. prescribe ☐ r. medication
☐ s. break out in a rash ☐ t. itchy ☐ u. insect bite
☐ v. have a prescription filled

```
1. アレルギー    2. 薬剤    3. くしゃみする    4. ～で苦しむ；～を患う    5. 鼻水
6. 虫刺され    7.（緊張、苦痛などの）除去・軽減    8. 寝違える    9. かゆい
10. 筋肉のけいれん；筋違い    11. 処方する    12.（病気・けがを）治す
13. 処方薬を調剤してもらう    14. ヒリヒリする；炎症を起こしている    15. 目薬
16. 発疹ができる    17. 薬剤師    18. 通路    19. 症状    20. 貼り薬    21. 花粉症
22.（薬が）～に効く
```

2 Comprehension Questions

 3-02, 03, 04

Listen to the three conversations and choose the best answer for each question.

(A) Conversation at a Pharmacy

Q1. What is Hiroshi looking for?

  a) something to heal his neck and something to help him sleep well
  b) some cold medicine and eye care goods
  c) medicine for his neck pain and eye drops

61

Q2. What is the most likely cause of Hiroshi's neck pain?

    a) He has a stiff neck and did not sleep well last night.

    b) He twisted his neck while sleeping last night.

    c) He didn't sleep well because of his itchy eyes.

    | have a stiff neck「首が凝っている」

(B) Conversation at a Pharmacy

Q3. Which of the following statements is NOT true?

    a) Yoko is looking for something for her hay fever.

    b) The pharmacist prescribes medication for her hay fever.

    c) Yoko is suffering from a runny nose.

(C) Seeing a Doctor

Q4. Which of the following statements is true?

    a) The doctor thinks Hiroshi has a broken leg.

    b) Hiroshi needs medication to help him sleep well.

    c) Hiroshi is suffering from red spots on his skin.

Q5. How should Hiroshi take the medication?

    a) He should take two tablets and a pill at bedtime.

    b) He should take two pills and one tablet after dinner.

    c) He should take two pills and one tablet after breakfast.

3 Dictation

CD 3-05, 06, 07

Fill in the blanks while listening to the conversations.

A. Conversation at a Pharmacy

Hiroshi: I'm looking for something to (^{1}) my neck pain.

Pharmacist: What happened?

Hiroshi: Well, I (^{2}) up with a crick in my neck. I may have (^{3}) wrong. It hurts.

Pharmacist: Umm. Why don't you try this product? It'll help (^{4}) your pain.

Hiroshi: Are they patches?

Pharmacist: Yes, this package contains three of them.

Hiroshi: Thank you. I think I'll try them. Also, I need eye drops. My eyes are (^{5}) and irritated.

Pharmacist: Eye care products are on aisle 5.

UNIT 11 Health Care

Hiroshi: Thanks.

B. Conversation at a Pharmacy

Yoko: Excuse me. I'm wondering if this medicine (6   ) for hay fever.
Pharmacist: No, this one is for allergies only. It gives some (7   ) but it's not very good for hay fever.
Yoko: Really? Could you recommend a better medicine?
Pharmacist: What are your symptoms?
Yoko: Sneezing and irritated eyes. Also, I'm (8   ) from a runny nose.
Pharmacist: I see. They sound like common symptoms of hay fever. This new medicine should work better. You may get (9   ), but that's not really serious. If it doesn't work, you should ask your doctor to (10   ) a stronger medication.
Yoko: I see. Thanks a lot.

C. Seeing a Doctor

Doctor: What seems to be the (11   )?
Hiroshi: My right leg (12   ) out in a (13   ) a week ago, and now it has (14   ) to my left leg. It's (15   ), and I have trouble sleeping well.
Doctor: I see. Let me see it. ... Ah, I think it's an insect (16   ). Don't worry. It's easy to cure.
Hiroshi: What a relief!
Doctor: I'll write a prescription for you. Take it to a (17   ) to have it filled.
Hiroshi: Okay, I will. Thank you, doctor.

[At a Pharmacy]
Hiroshi: Could you (18   ) my prescription?
Pharmacist: Okay. It will take about 15 minutes or so.
Hiroshi: All right.

[15 minutes later]
Hiroshi: Can I pick up my medication?
Pharmacist: Yes, it's ready. Take two of these pills and have one of these (19   ) after breakfast.
Hiroshi: All right. Thanks.

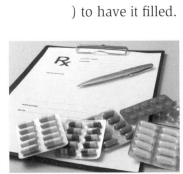

63

4 Related Dialogs 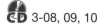 3-08, 09, 10

Listen to the three dialogs and choose the best answer for each question.

Dialog One

Question: **Where is this conversation taking place?**

    a. at a dental clinic   **b.** at a medical clinic   **c.** at a restaurant

| filling 「詰め物」　fall out 「抜け落ちる」

Dialog Two

Question: **Which of the following foods should he avoid?**

    a. fried chicken   **b.** oysters   **c.** tuna

Dialog Three

Question: **Which of the following symptoms did she NOT mention?**

    a. chills   **b.** sneeze   **c.** sore throat

| vomit 「おう吐する；吐く」

5 Useful Expressions 3-11

Listen and write the sentences.

1. ....

2. ....

3. ....

4. ....

UNIT 11 | Health Care

6 Substitution Drills

 3-12, 13, 14

Complete the substitution drill in the following way.

(1) I'm looking for <u>something</u> to <u>heal my neck pain</u>.

> **Example:** a good medicine – cure my stomachache
> ➡ I'm looking for a good medicine to cure my stomachache.

a) a good medicine – cure my stomachache
b) something – help ease my dry eyes
c) heat patches – relieve my backache

ease = relieve「和らげる；軽減する」

(2) <u>I'm</u> suffering from <u>a runny nose</u>.

> **Example:** My sister is – a splitting headache
> ➡ My sister is suffering from a splitting headache.

a) My sister is – a splitting headache
b) He was – a throbbing toothache
c) We've been – jet lag

splitting headache「頭が割れるような頭痛」 throbbing toothache「ズキズキする歯痛」
jet lag「時差ボケ」

(3) They <u>sound</u> like <u>common symptoms of hay fever</u>.

> **Example:** seem – general signs of diabetes
> ➡ They seem like general signs of diabetes.

a) seem – general signs of diabetes
b) look – typical symptoms of food poisoning
c) sound – usual symptoms of pneumonia

diabetes [dàiəbíːtiːz]「糖尿病」 food poisoning「食中毒」 pneumonia [nuːmóuniə]「肺炎」

7 Translation

Put the following Japanese sentences into English.

1. あなたは寝違えたのかもしれませんね。

2. この貼り薬を試してみてはどうでしょうか。痛みが和らぎますよ。

_____

3. この薬は頭痛に効くのでしょうか。

_____

4. この処方薬を調剤してください。

_____

8 Vocabulary

Fill in the blanks with the words and phrases provided below.

1. I have a _____.　　　　　　　　　頭痛がします。
2. I have a _____ nose.　　　　　　鼻詰まりです。
3. I have a _____ nose.　　　　　　鼻水が出ます。
4. I have a bad _____.　　　　　　ひどい咳（せき）が出ます。
5. I have a _____ throat.　　　　　のどが痛いです。
6. I feel _____.　　　　　　　　　めまいがします。
7. I'm _____.　　　　　　　　　　便秘しています。
8. I have _____.　　　　　　　　　下痢をしています。
9. I feel like _____.　　　　　　　吐き気がします。
10. I have no _____.　　　　　　　食欲がありません。
11. I'm _____ cedar pollen.　　　スギ花粉アレルギーです。
12. I'm having my _____ now.　　生理中です。
13. I have a _____.　　　　　　　二日酔いです。
14. My leg _____.　　　　　　　　脚が痛みます。
15. I think I have a _____.　　　　虫歯だと思います。
16. A dental _____ has fallen out.　歯の詰め物がとれました。
17. I have a _____ all over my body.　体中に湿疹が出ています。
18. I _____ my ankle while skiing.　スキーで足首を捻挫しました。
19. I _____ my neck while I was sleeping.　寝違えました。
20. I have _____ fever.　　　　　　花粉症です。

hurts	sore	runny	filling	stuffy
twisted	period	sprained	rash	throwing up
hay	allergic to	cough	appetite	constipated
hangover	cavity	dizzy	diarrhea [dàiəríːə]	headache

UNIT 12 Shopping

1 Pre-Listening Exercise

Guess what these words mean and match the appropriate meaning given in Japanese.

- a. try on
- b. fit
- c. tight
- d. instep
- e. loose
- f. come in ~
- g. way too much
- h. price range
- i. at most
- j. hobo bag
- k. affordable
- l. durable
- m. on sale
- n. reduce to ~
- o. gift-wrap

> 1. 手頃な価格の　2.〈商品が〉(〜の形で) 売られている　3. 価格帯　4. ギフト用に包装する　5. 最大限でも　6. 特価で　7. 丈夫な；長持ちする　8. 〜まで引き下げる　9. 足の甲　10. ぴったり合う　11. 試着する；履いてみる　12. きつい　13. はるかに（価格が）高い　14. ゆるい　15. 三日月型をしたショルダーバッグ

2 Comprehension Questions

 3-15, 16

(A) *Listen to the conversation between Hiroshi and a clerk at a shoe store and choose the best answer for each question.*

Q1. Which of the following statements is true?

   a) The first shoes are a little too small at the instep.
   b) The second shoes are a little too big at the instep.
   c) Hiroshi decided to buy the third pair of shoes in black.

Q2. How much does Hiroshi pay in sales tax?

   a) $8.16
   b) $125.50
   c) $133.66

67

(B) **Listen to the conversation between Yoko and a clerk at a department store and choose the best answer for each question.**

Q3. **What does the clerk think about the hobo bag?**
   a) It's expensive.
   b) It will last a long time.
   c) It's a bit old-fashioned.

Q4. **How much was the hobo bag a week ago?**
   a) $223.50   b) $228.00   c) $136.80

3 Dictation

 3-17, 18

Fill in the blanks while listening to the dialogs.

A. At a Shoe Shop

Hiroshi: Excuse me. Could you help me?
   Clerk: Yes, what (¹   ) I do for you?
Hiroshi: Well, I'm interested in these shoes.
   Clerk: Do you want to (²   ) them on?
Hiroshi: Yes, please.
   Clerk: All right. ... Here you go.
   [*He tries them on.*]
   Clerk: How do they (³   )?
Hiroshi: I think they are a little too (⁴   ) at the (⁵   ).
   Clerk: All right. Why don't you try these on?
   [*He tries them on.*]
Hiroshi: They fit my instep, but I'm afraid they are a little (⁶   ) in the heel.
   Clerk: Okay. ... [*She offers a different pair.*] These should fit.
Hiroshi: Yeah, you're right. They fit me perfectly. Do you have these in different colors?
   Clerk: Yes, this particular style (⁷   ) in gray, brown, and black.
Hiroshi: I'll take the brown ones.
   Clerk: All right. That's $(⁸   ) plus 6.5 percent sales tax. That comes to

$(⁹   ). Will that be cash or (¹⁰   )?

Hiroshi: Do you accept Mastercard?

Clerk: Sure.

B. Buying a Gift at a Department Store

Clerk: May I help you?

Yoko: Yes, I'm (¹¹   ) for a nice gift for my sister. Could you recommend something?

Clerk: All right. How about this bracelet?

Yoko: No, I don't think she cares for bracelets.

Clerk: In that case, how about this necklace? It's quite reasonable.

Yoko: I like the style. How much is it?

Clerk: It's $(¹²   ).

Yoko: I'm afraid that's (¹³   ) too much.

Clerk: Oh, may I ask what your price range is?

Yoko: I'm thinking around $150 at most.

Clerk: All right. How about this hobo bag? This is quite (¹⁴   ) and (¹⁵   ). I'm sure your sister would love it.

Yoko: Umm. How much is it?

Clerk: It was $228 a week ago, but it's on sale now and the price is reduced to $(¹⁶   ) plus tax.

Yoko: Okay, I'll take it.

Clerk: All right. ... Your total comes to $(¹⁷   ). Cash or credit card?

Yoko: Credit card. Could you gift-wrap it for me?

Clerk: Gift-wrapping is (¹⁸   ) on the 8th floor.

4 Related Dialogs

 3-19, 20, 21

Listen to the three dialogs and choose the best answer for each question.

Dialog One

Question: **Which of the following statements is true?**

a. The woman wants the clerk to find something.

b. The woman thanks the clerk for looking around.

c. The woman needs no help from the clerk.

Dialog Two

Question: **How much is the woman's total before tax?**

    a. $25.90   **b.** $46.90   **c.** $59.85

| ad = advertisement「広告」

Dialog Three

Question: **How does the man pay?**

    a. with cash   **b.** by credit card   **c.** with cash and a credit card

| the rest「残り（の代金）」

5 Useful Expressions

 3-22

Listen and write the sentences.

1. ....
2. ....
3. ....
4. ....

6 Substitution Drills

 3-23, 24, 25

Complete the substitution drill in the following way.

(1) **I think** they are a little too **tight at the instep**.

> **Example:** I'm afraid – loose in the heel
> ➡ I'm afraid they are a little too loose in the heel.

    a) I'm afraid – loose in the heel
    b) I think – wide for my feet
    c) I believe – small for your feet

UNIT 12 | Shopping

(2) Do you **have these** in **different colors?**

> **Example:** carry this sweater – different sizes
> ➡ Do you carry this sweater in different sizes?

a) carry this sweater – different sizes

b) have different styles – the same color

c) have other designs – the same price range

(3) **I'm looking for a nice gift for my sister.**

> **Example:** an affordable scarf – my sister
> ➡ I'm looking for an affordable scarf for my sister.

a) an affordable scarf – my sister

b) a durable T-shirt – my friend

c) a user-friendly smartphone – my father

| user-friendly「使いやすい」

7 Translation

Put the following Japanese sentences into English.

1. このジーンズは君にきっと似合うと思います。

_____

2. このTシャツにします。ギフト用に包んでください。

_____

3. 私のiPhoneに入れるプリペイドのSIMカードを探しています。

_____

4. このセーターは胸（chest）回りが少しきついです。

_____

5. この靴はすごく安価で長持ちします。

_____

71

🌐 8 Vocabulary

Fill in the blank with the words provided below.

1. Do you _____ the same one in different colors? 　　同じもので違う色のものはありますか。

2. Can I have a _____ on this sweater? 　　このセーターの払い戻しを受けられますか。

3. Can you _____ it for something different? 　　違うものと交換していただけますか。

4. The _____ room is over there. 　　試着室はあちらです。

5. It's too _____ for me. 　　少し派手すぎます。

6. I think it's a bit _____ for me. 　　ちょっと地味だと思います。

7. Please _____ your time. 　　どうぞごゆっくり。

8. Is it possible to have it _____? 　　配達してもらえますか。

9. Could you give me a _____ on this? 　　これを値引きしてもらえませんか。

10. You didn't give me the _____ change. 　　お釣りが間違っています。

11. It's a little _____ around my neck. 　　首回りが少しきついです。

12. I'm afraid it's way over my _____. 　　残念ながら、予算をはるかにオーバーしています。

13. I'm looking for _____ a little less expensive. 　　もう少し安いものを探しているのですが。

14. Is this _____? 　　丈夫ですか（長持ちしますか）。

15. Does it _____ after washing? 　　洗ったら縮みますか。

16. Is there a _____ around here? 　　この近くにお手洗いはありますか。

17. This is a little too _____ around my waist. 　　これは、ウエスト回りが少しゆるすぎます。

18. These shoes are out of _____. 　　この靴は在庫がありません。

discount	shrink	fitting	durable	budget	take
restroom	something	flashy	carry	loose	exchange
stock	delivered	quiet	right	tight	refund

72

Some important statistics

* Seven out of 10 complaining customers will do business with again you if you resolve the complaint in their favor.
* Of complaining customers, 95 percent will do business with you again if you resolve the complaint at the first contact.
* On average, a satisfied complainer will tell five people about their problem and how it was solved.
* It costs six times more to attract new customers that it does to retain current ones.

Making Complaints

1 Pre-Listening Exercise

Guess what these words mean and match the appropriate meaning given in Japanese.

- ☐ a. hallway
- ☐ b. ~ or something
- ☐ c. connect to ~
- ☐ d. specific
- ☐ e. unstable
- ☐ f. frequently
- ☐ g. complaint
- ☐ h. chef
- ☐ i. over easy
- ☐ j. scrambled eggs
- ☐ k. I've had it.

> 1. ～につながる　2. 頻繁に　3. 具体的な　4. (卵が) 両面焼き半熟の　5. スクランブルエッグ　6. もううんざりだ。　7. 苦情　8. ～か何か　9. シェフ, コック長　10. 不安定な　11. 廊下

2 Comprehension Questions

 3-26, 27

(A) Listen to the conversation between Hiroshi and a hotel clerk and choose the best answer for each question.

Q1. What's Hiroshi's first complaint?

　a) The people in room 208 are very noisy.

　b) The people in room 230 are having a party.

　c) Hiroshi couldn't go to sleep until 2 o'clock.

Q2. What's the second complaint?

　a) Wi-Fi service is not available in his room.

　b) His smartphone cannot connect to the Wi-Fi.

　c) His smartphone doesn't stay connected to the Wi-Fi.

73

(B) Listen to the conversation between Yoko and a waiter and choose the best answer for each question.

Q3. What time did Yoko order?

    a) 9:10   b) 9:20   c) 9:30

Q4. What did Yoko order?

    a) pancakes, scrambled eggs, and tomato juice

    b) French toast, scrambled eggs, and tomato juice

    c) French toast, over-easy eggs, and grapefruit juice

3 Dictation

 3-28, 29

Fill in the blanks while listening to the dialogs.

A. Complaining in a Hotel

Hiroshi: Hello. There are a couple of things I'm (¹   ) about.

Clerk: I see, sir.

Hiroshi: Last night, the people (²   ) the hallway had a party or something and were making noise till (³   ) in the morning. I could hardly sleep. Could you please tell them to be more (⁴   )?

Clerk: I'm very sorry, sir. I'll tell them that. What's their room number?

Hiroshi: Room (⁵   ). Also, my smartphone doesn't seem to connect to the Wi-Fi in my room.

Clerk: Could you be more (⁶   ) about the problem?

Hiroshi: Well, the Wi-Fi signal is very weak and (⁷   ). My smartphone frequently loses the signal.

Clerk: I'm sorry, sir. Unfortunately, some smartphones have (⁸   ) connecting to the in-room Wi-Fi. But free Wi-Fi is also (⁹   ) in the lobby. That should work.

UNIT 13 Making Complaints

B. Complaining in a Restaurant

Yoko: Excuse me. My meal (¹⁰   ) come yet. I ordered it about 20 minutes ago.

Waiter: I'm very sorry. I'll check your order with the chef.

Yoko: Please hurry. I have an (¹¹   ) with my friend at 10:00, and I have only (¹²   ) minutes left.

Waiter: I'll be right back with your meal.

[*a few minutes later*]

Waiter: Thank you for waiting. Here's your meal.

Yoko: Excuse me. This isn't (¹³   ) I ordered.

Waiter: What was your order?

Yoko: I ordered French toast and two eggs over easy, not pancakes and scrambled eggs. I didn't order tomato juice either. I ordered (¹⁴   ) juice.

Waiter: I'm very sorry. I'll be right back.

Yoko: No, that (¹⁵   ) be necessary. I've had it. I can't wait any longer. Just cancel my order, will you?

4 Related Dialogs

 3-30, 31, 32

Listen to the three dialogs and choose the best answer for each question.

Dialog One

Question: **What is the problem?**

    a. Tomoko didn't get the wake-up call that she asked for.

    b. Tomoko wanted to wake up at 6:30 instead of 5:30.

    c. Tomoko mistakenly got wake-up calls on two consecutive days.

wake-up call「モーニングコール」 supervisor「管理者」 consecutive「連続した」

Dialog Two

Question: **What is the woman complaining about?**

    a. She can smell tobacco smoke in the hallway.

    b. She wants a smoking room.

    c. Her room smells of cigarettes.

stand「我慢する」 smell of~「〜のにおいがする」

75

Dialog Three

Question: **What will the clerk do for her?**

    a. He'll get someone to clean her room right away.

    b. He'll find a clean room for her immediately.

    c. He'll have her wait so that he can clean her room.

| immediately 「すぐに」

5 Useful Expressions

Listen and write the sentences.

1. ....

2. ....

3. ....

4. ....

6 Substitution Drills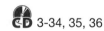

Complete the substitution drill in the following way.

(1) I ordered <u>French toast</u>, not <u>pancakes</u>.

> **Example:** two eggs over easy – scrambled eggs
> ➡ I ordered two eggs over easy, not scrambled eggs.

    a) two eggs over easy – scrambled eggs

    b) a glass of orange juice – tomato juice

    c) a roast beef sandwich – a double fishburger

UNIT 13 Making Complaints

(2) Unfortunately, some guests <u>don't follow</u> the <u>no smoking policy</u>.

> **Example:** often ignore – no cooking policy
>
> ➡ Unfortunately, some guests often ignore the no cooking policy.

a) often ignore – no cooking policy

b) sometimes take no notice of – no pets allowed policy

c) pay no attention to – quiet hours policy

(3) I'll <u>give you a call</u> when <u>the room is ready</u>.

> **Example:** notify you – the room is cleaned
>
> ➡ I'll notify you when the room is cleaned.

a) notify you – the room is cleaned

b) let you know – your turn comes

c) send someone to pick up your baggage – you give us a call

| notify「知らせる」 turn「順番」

🌐 7 Translation

Put the following Japanese sentences into English.

1. 私の部屋について問題があるのですが。

_____

2. 隣の宿泊客があまりにうるさいので、まったく寝られませんでした。

_____

3. 私のスマホが Wi-Fi につながりません。

_____

4. 私が注文したのは、コーヒーではなくてコーラです。それにこの魚料理は注文していません。

_____

5. もううんざりです。私の注文を取り消してください。

_____

77

8 Reading for Information

Read the following advice regarding how to handle guest complaints and answer the questions.

Guest Complaints

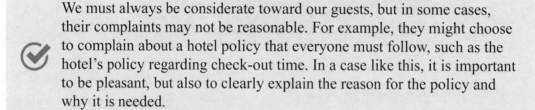 We must always be considerate toward our guests, but in some cases, their complaints may not be reasonable. For example, they might choose to complain about a hotel policy that everyone must follow, such as the hotel's policy regarding check-out time. In a case like this, it is important to be pleasant, but also to clearly explain the reason for the policy and why it is needed.

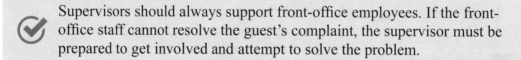 Supervisors should always support front-office employees. If the front-office staff cannot resolve the guest's complaint, the supervisor must be prepared to get involved and attempt to solve the problem.

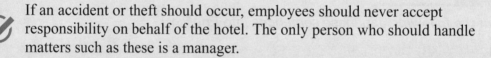 If an accident or theft should occur, employees should never accept responsibility on behalf of the hotel. The only person who should handle matters such as these is a manager.

1. If the guests do not follow a hotel policy, what should you do?

2. What does the author recommend when a front-office staff member cannot handle the guest's complaints?

3. If a guest has his or her wallet stolen, what should hotel employees NOT do?

UNIT 14 Dealing with Problems

1 Pre-Listening Exercise

Guess what these words mean and match the appropriate meaning given in Japanese.

☐ a. missing   ☐ b. carousel [kǽrəsél]   ☐ c. baggage claim area
☐ d. baggage claim tag   ☐ e. wheel   ☐ f. sticker   ☐ g. deliver
☐ h. cell phone number   ☐ i. lost and found   ☐ j. turn in   ☐ k. leather
☐ l. kitchenware   ☐ m. Don't panic.   ☐ n. notepad

```
1. 携帯電話番号    2. 配達する    3. 手荷物引換証    4. うろたえるな。落ち着け。
5. メモ帳    6. 手荷物受取所    7. 台所用品    8. 革製の    9. 遺失物取扱所
10. 車輪    11. 届ける；提出する    12. 回転式コンベヤー    13. 紛失した
14. ステッカー，シール
```

2 Comprehension Questions

 3-37, 38

(A) Listen to the conversation about Hiroshi's missing baggage and choose the best answer for each question.

Q1. Which of the following statements is true?

　　a) Hiroshi will be staying at the Day's Inn for one night.

　　b) Hiroshi will be staying at the Comfort Inn for two nights.

　　c) Hiroshi will be staying at the Ramada Inn for three nights.

Q2. Which of the following best describes Hiroshi's suitcase?

　　a) a brown suitcase tied with a blue and red belt

　　b) a blue suitcase tied with a black and white belt

　　c) a silver suitcase tied with a yellow and white belt

(B) Listen to the conversation about Yoko's missing bag and choose the best answer for each question.

Q3. Which of the following descriptions best fits Yoko's bag?

　　a) It's a large shoulder bag with her camera and smartphone in it.

　　b) It's a black handbag with her passport and tablet in it.

　　c) It's a pink leather bag with her camera and notepad in it.

Q4. Where is lost and found?

　　a) on the second floor in front of the shoe department

　　b) on the third floor next to the furniture department

　　c) on the fourth floor behind the kitchenware department

3 Dictation

3-39, 40

Fill in the blanks while listening to the dialogs.

A. Missing Baggage

Hiroshi: Excuse me. My baggage seems to be missing. It hasn't come out onto the carousel.

　Clerk: Did you check all the baggage at the baggage (¹　　　) area?

Hiroshi: Yes, I did, but I couldn't find it.

　Clerk: Do you have a baggage claim (²　　　) with you?

Hiroshi: Yes. It should be in my bag. ... Here it is.

　Clerk: Could you (³　　　) your baggage? What kind is it?

Hiroshi: It's a pretty large (⁴　　　) suitcase with wheels and a (⁵　　　) and white belt around it. There are also several stickers on both sides of it. Could you check for its location right now?

....

　Clerk: All right. Just a moment, please.

Hiroshi: Thank you.

　Clerk: I'm afraid we can't find your suitcase.

Hiroshi: Really? What should I do now?

　Clerk: Don't panic. We'll find it ... Please fill out this form. Where should we (⁶　　　) it when we locate it?

UNIT 14 Dealing with Problems

Hiroshi: To the Ramada Inn. Please call me when you find it. I'll be staying there for three nights. Here is my (^{7}) phone number.

Clerk: All right. We'll let you know and deliver it to your hotel as soon as we find it.

Hiroshi: Thanks a lot.

B. Lost and Found

[*Yoko makes a phone call to a department store.*]

Clerk A: Marshall's Department Store. May I help you?

Yoko: Yes. I might have (^{8}) my bag at your store. I'm wondering if someone has turned it in.

Clerk A: Let me (^{9}) you to our lost and found department. One moment, please.

Clerk B: Lost and found. May I help you?

Yoko: Hello? My name is Yoko Iwai. I think I left my bag at your store earlier today. It's a small shoulder bag made of (^{10}) leather. My camera and (^{11}) are in it.

Clerk B: Yes, someone did turn in a shoulder bag like that.

Yoko: That's a relief!

Clerk B: Are you coming to pick it up?

Yoko: Yes, I'll be there within an hour. (^{12}) which floor is your lost and found located?

Clerk B: We're on the (^{13}) floor, in the back of the (^{14}) department.

4 Related Dialogs

CD 3-41, 42, 43

Listen to the three dialogs and choose the best answer for each question.

Dialog One

Question: **What happened?**

    a. He had his wallet stolen.

    b. He dropped his wallet.

    c. His wallet is missing.

| calm down「落ち着く」　pick one's pocket「すり（窃盗）を行う」　straight away「直ちに」

81

Dialog Two

Question: **Which of the following best describes her bag?**

    a. a black handbag   **b.** a leather shoulder bag

    c. a brown leather tote bag

Dialog Three

Question: **What is the problem with his suitcase?**

    a. It is badly damaged.   **b.** It is missing.   **c.** Someone stole it.

| be cracked「ひびが入る」 repair「修理」

5 Useful Expressions

 3-44

Listen and write the sentences.

1. ....

2. ....

3. ....

4. ....

6 Substitution Drills

 3-45, 46, 47

Complete the substitution drill in the following way.

(1) It's a <u>large suitcase</u> with <u>wheels</u>.

> **Example:** black hard suitcase – a handle and wheels
> ➡ It's a black hard suitcase with a handle and wheels.

    a) black hard suitcase – a handle and wheels

    b) large blue soft suitcase – a black and yellow belt around it

    c) tiny backpack – my name tag

| tiny = small   name tag「名札」

UNIT 14 Dealing with Problems

(2) We'll <u>let you know and deliver it to your hotel</u> as soon as we find it.

> **Example:** inform you – the moment we find your baggage
> ➡ We'll inform you the moment we find your baggage.

a) inform you – the moment we find your baggage

b) report to you – when we have further information

c) give you a call – when someone has turned in your backpack

❙ the moment = as soon as「～するとすぐに」

(3) I'm wondering if <u>someone has turned it in</u>.

> **Example:** He's wondering – you've found his smartphone
> ➡ He's wondering if you've found his smartphone.

a) He's wondering – you've found his smartphone

b) I'm wondering – you're available on Saturday afternoon

c) We're wondering – you could help us enter data into the computer

❙ enter data into ~「データを～に入力する」

7 Translation

Put the following Japanese sentences into English.

1. 私のスーツケースが回転式コンベヤーに出てきません。

_____

2. パスポートを紛失してしまいました。どうしたらいいですか。

_____

3. 私が本を買う時に、財布がないことに気づきました。

_____

4. 買い物をしている間に、誰かが私にすりを働いたようです。

_____

5. これ見てください。私のスーツケースにひびが入り、ロックも壊れています。

_____

83

🌐 8 Reading for Information

Read the following safety information and write T if the statement is true and F if it is not true.

SAFETY TIPS FOR GUESTS

1. Never answer the door without checking to see who is there. If the person claims to be an employee, call the Front Desk to confirm.

2. If you go back to your room late in the evening, always use the hotel's main entrance. In particular, be observant and look around before entering parking lots.

3. Make sure that your door is securely closed whenever you are in your room and that you use all of the locks provided.

4. Take good care with your guest room key. Don't display it in public or leave it in a place where it can be easily stolen, such as on a restaurant table or at the swimming pool.

5. Avoid attracting attention by displaying large amounts of cash or expensive jewelry.

6. Never allow a stranger to enter your room.

7. Make sure all your valuable items are kept in the hotel safe deposit box.

8. Never leave valuables unattended in your car.

9. Make sure to lock sliding glass doors or windows as well as connecting room doors.

10. Report any suspicious activities to the management.

> confirm ~「～を確かめる」 be observant「よく注意を払ってください」 valuables「貴重品」
> safe deposit box「貸金庫」 leave ~ unattended「～を放置する」 suspicious「不審な」

1. _____ Open the door whenever the hotel employees ask you to.

2. _____ Parking lots in the evening can be dangerous, so be very careful.

3. _____ When you are in your room, close the door and use all the locks.

4. _____ Someone may steal your guest room key, so don't leave it lying around.

5. _____ It is not safe to show all your dollar bills in public.

6. _____ You can leave your expensive laptop in your car as long as it is unseen.

7. _____ If you see someone doing something suspicious, you should call the police.

84

UNIT 15
At the Airport

1 Pre-Listening Exercise

Guess what these words mean and match the appropriate meaning given in Japanese.

☐ **a.** aisle [áil] seat   ☐ **b.** check-in counter   ☐ **c.** scale
☐ **d.** baggage allowance   ☐ **e.** name tag   ☐ **f.** attach   ☐ **g.** boarding pass
☐ **h.** departure   ☐ **i.** bound for ~   ☐ **j.** be delayed   ☐ **k.** due to ~
☐ **l.** connecting flight   ☐ **m.** can't make it   ☐ **n.** LAX   ☐ **o.** inconvenience

```
1. 接続便   2. 重量計   3. ~行きの   4. 搭乗手続きカウンター   5. ロサンゼルス国
際空港の空港コード   6. 不便，迷惑   7. 出発   8. 間に合わない   9. 遅れる
10. ~のため；~が原因で   11. 名札   12. 取り付ける   13. 通路側の席
14. （無料）手荷物許容量   15. 搭乗券
```

2 Comprehension Questions

 3-48, 49

(A) Listen to the conversation between Hiroshi and a check-in clerk and choose the best answer for each question.

Q1. Which flight will Hiroshi be on?

    a) AA flight 515   **b)** AA flight 550   **c)** AA flight 150

Q2. What's the weight allowance for each suitcase?

    a) 15 pounds   **b)** 15 kilograms   **c)** 50 pounds

85

(B) Listen to the conversation between Yoko and an airline employee and choose the best answer for each question.

Q3. Which flight will be delayed?

    a) Flight 237   **b)** Flight 372   **c)** Flight 723

Q4. Which flight will Yoko be taking from Los Angeles to San Francisco?

    a) American Airlines flight 723

    b) United Airlines flight 1863

    c) United Airlines flight 447

3 Dictation

 3-50, 51

Fill in the blanks while listening to the dialogs.

A. At a Check-in Counter

Hiroshi: Is this the check-in counter for (¹   ) flight (²   ) to Tokyo?

Clerk: Yes, it is. May I see your passport and ticket, please?

Hiroshi: Sure. Here you are.

Clerk: Thank you, sir. Do you have any baggage to check in?

Hiroshi: Yes, these two suitcases.

Clerk: Okay. Would you (³   ) both of them on the scale?

Hiroshi: Sure. What's the baggage allowance?

Clerk: It's (⁴   ) pounds for each piece. Yours are all right. Do you have any carry-ons?

Hiroshi: Yes, this small bag.

Clerk: Please fill out this name (⁵   ) and attach it to your bag.

Hiroshi: Okay. And I'd like an aisle seat, please.

Clerk: I'm sorry, but there aren't any aisle seats (⁶   ). Would you like me to put you in a window seat?

Hiroshi: Yes, please.

Clerk: All right. Here is your boarding (⁷   ) and your baggage claim tag.

Hiroshi: Thank you. Is my flight on time?

Clerk: Yes, it leaves at 3:45.

Hiroshi: Which gate should I go to?

Clerk: Go to the international (⁸   ) lounge. Your flight will be leaving from Gate 35. Please be there 30 minutes before departure.

| pound 「ポンド」約 0.45 キロ

B. Delayed Flight

[*Announcement*]
Flight (⁹   ) bound for Los Angeles will be delayed one hour. Boarding will take (¹⁰   ) at 7:30 a.m.

Yoko: Excuse me. I've just heard flight (¹¹   ) has been delayed.

Clerk: I'm sorry, but that flight is delayed about one hour (¹²   ) to a mechanical problem.

Yoko: Really? I have a connecting flight at Los Angeles. I'm afraid I can't (¹³   ) it. What should I do?

Clerk: Please (¹⁴   ) down. Maybe, I can find another flight from Los Angeles for you. May I see your ticket?

Yoko: Here it is.

Clerk: Let's see. You are now (¹⁵   ) on United Airlines flight 1863 leaving LAX at 10:42 a.m. I'll put you on UA (¹⁶   ) to San Francisco. It'll be leaving at 12:25 p.m.

Yoko: What about my baggage?

Clerk: Don't worry. We'll see that it's transferred to UA447.

Yoko: Good.

Clerk: We're sorry for the inconvenience.

4 Related Monolog/Dialogs  3-52, 53, 54

Listen to the airport announcement and two dialogs and choose the best answer for each question.

Monolog One

Question: **What happened to flight 205?**
   a. It has been delayed due to engine trouble.
   b. It will be delayed due to fog.
   c. It won't take off until 2:05.

Dialog One

Question: **Which flight is she taking?**

　　a. United flight 502　　b. United flight 92　　c. United flight 340

Dialog Two

Question: **Which of the following statements is true?**

　　a. Passengers in economy class are not allowed to check in more than two pieces of baggage.

　　b. Shipping a suitcase as unaccompanied baggage is more expensive than the excess baggage charge.

　　c. Shipping a suitcase as unaccompanied baggage is as costly as the excess baggage charge.

| excess baggage charge「超過手荷物料金」　unaccompanied baggage「別送手荷物」

5 Useful Expressions

 3-55

Listen and write the sentences.

1. ....
2. ....
3. ....
4. ....

6 Substitution Drills

 3-56, 57, 58

Complete the substitution drill in the following way.

(1) Would you like me to <u>put you in a window seat</u>?

> **Example:** put you in an aisle seat
> ➡ Would you like me to put you in an aisle seat?

88

UNIT 15 At the Airport

a) put you in an aisle seat

b) put you on the waiting list

c) seat you two together

(2) Your <u>flight</u> will be leaving <u>from Gate 35</u>.

> **Example:** bus – at 10:30
> ➡ Your bus will be leaving at 10:30.

a) bus – at 10:30

b) train – from track 6

c) flight – in an hour

(3) The flight <u>is delayed one hour</u> due to <u>a mechanical problem</u>.

> **Example:** will be delayed for some time – technical difficulties
> ➡ The flight will be delayed for some time due to technical difficulties.

a) will be delayed for some time – technical difficulties

b) is expected to be delayed – minor engine trouble

c) was canceled – a heavy snowstorm

🌐 7 Translation

Put the following Japanese sentences into English.

1. 日本航空260便は18番ゲートから午後12：30に出発します。

_____

2. この名札に記入して、バッグに取り付けてください。

_____

3. 通路側の席をお願いします。

_____

4. 吹雪のため、35便ニューヨーク行きは欠航になりました。

_____

5. 技術的な問題（technical difficulties）のため、318便東京行きは1時間ほど遅れています。

_____

89

🌐 8 Reading for Information

Read the following information on flight delays and cancellations and write T if the statement is true and F if it is not true.

Delays and Cancellations

Before going to the airport, confirm that your flight is leaving on time by double-checking the airline's website. It is possible to set up flight status alerts that can be sent directly to your cell phone. Many airlines will offer this service. If not, you can use a website such as FlightStats.com.

Always remember that airlines are under no obligation to compensate passengers for flights that have been delayed or canceled. There are no federal laws requiring them to do this, and so policies will differ depending on the carrier. Most airlines will try to get you a seat on the next available flight. In some cases, the airline will pay for meals or a hotel stay if your plane is delayed, so be sure to ask about this.

In cases where the delay is caused by bad weather or other conditions beyond their control, some airlines will offer no amenities. The only time that compensation is legally required by law is if an airline bumps you from a flight that it has oversold. Although airlines are under no legal obligation to inform passengers about the causes for flight delays, many of them are now setting up their own programs to provide this service.

> flight status alert「フライトの状況通知」 compensate for ~「～の補償をする」 carrier「航空会社」 amenity「快適さ（を提供するもの）」この場合では食事やホテルを指す bump from a flight「フライトの予約が取り消される」

---

1. _____ Before you leave for the airport, make sure to have your cell phone with you.

2. _____ The airline's website provides information on whether your flight is leaving on time.

3. _____ To arrange flight status alerts, you can send your cell phone to the airlines.

4. _____ Information on flight status will be sent to your cell phone once you book an air ticket.

5. _____ Airlines are required to provide passengers with meals and hotel stays if their flight is canceled.

6. _____ Many airlines will not book you on another flight if your flight is canceled.

7. _____ Airlines are required by law to provide meals and hotels if a flight delay is caused by conditions beyond their control.

8. _____ The law requires airlines to compensate you if they cannot find you a seat on a flight you have booked.

TEXT PRODUCTION STAFF

edited by	編集
Eiichi Tamura	田村 栄一

cover design by	表紙デザイン
in-print	インプリント

text design by	本文デザイン
in-print	インプリント

CD PRODUCTION STAFF

narrated by	吹き込み者
Ilana Labourene (AmerE)	イラーナ・ラボリン（アメリカ英語）
Dominic Allen (AmerE)	ドミニク・アレン（アメリカ英語）
Jack Merluzzi (AmerE)	ジャック・マルージー（アメリカ英語）
Rachel Walzer (AmerE)	レイチェル・ウォルツァー（アメリカ英語）

Travel English at Your Fingertips-Revised Edition-
実用観光英語―改訂新版―

2019年1月20日　初版発行
2024年2月10日　第7刷発行

著　　者　　島田 拓司
　　　　　　Bill Benfield

発 行 者　　佐野 英一郎

発 行 所　　株式会社 成 美 堂
　　　　　　〒101-0052　東京都千代田区神田小川町3-22
　　　　　　TEL 03-3291-2261　FAX 03-3293-5490
　　　　　　https://www.seibido.co.jp

印 刷・製 本　倉敷印刷株式会社

ISBN 978-4-7919-7185-5　　　　　　　　　　　　　Printed in Japan

・落丁・乱丁本はお取り替えします。
・本書の無断複写は、著作権上の例外を除き著作権侵害となります。